Economic Transformat Sub-Saharan Africa

Sub-Saharan Africa is vastly diverse, and the 49 countries of the region range significantly in terms of population, size and economic scale. The region also differs in topography, climate, history, culture, languages and political systems. Given this vast diversity, it is, accordingly, difficult to draw general conclusions about the continent's economic performance as a whole. Additionally, the lack of current statistics for several countries makes it difficult to make accurate assessments of economic conditions. Nevertheless, some broad comparisons can be made. Of the world's developing areas, sub-Saharan Africa has the worst record in virtually all of the most important social and economic indicators: the region has the lowest gross national income per head; the lowest life expectancy at birth; the lowest youth literacy rate; the highest rate of adult HIV infection; and the highest number of children not living past five years of age.

This volume begins by examining recent economic developments and trends. It then looks at the major economic constraints the region has faced in recent years, breaking down those constraints as either 'external' (e.g. terms of trade) over which the individual countries have but limited control, or 'internal' (e.g. governance and economic policy), over which there is more control. The book concludes by arguing that, despite the notable challenges cited above, sub-Saharan Africa is poised for a transformation, based on closer regional economic co-operation, a growing middle class, increased demand for locally produced goods and services, and a young population.

Donald L. Sparks, PhD, is Emeritus Professor of International Economics at the Citadel in Charleston, South Carolina, USA and a university lecturer in International Business at the Management Center Innsbruck, Austria.

Europa Introduction to...

The Focus titles in this series build on the unparalleled worldwide coverage of The Europa World Year Book and its associated regional surveys: Africa South of the Sahara; Central and South-Eastern Europe; Eastern Europe, Russia and Central Asia; The Far East and Australasia; The Middle East and North Africa; South America, Central America and the Caribbean; South Asia; The USA and Canada; and Western Europe, also available online at www.europa-world.com. Books in the series provide students, postgraduates, academics, professionals and researchers with up-to-date, balanced, authoritative and concise introductions to topics in the Europa core areas of country-specific contemporary politics and economics, and regional and international affairs. Volumes in the series, authored by experts, present a factual overview in a concise format, offering readers the opportunity rapidly to research current issues.

Italy's Contemporary Politics
James L. Newell

Economic Transformation in Sub-Saharan Africa
The Way Forward
Donald L. Sparks

Economic Transformation in Sub-Saharan Africa

The Way Forward

Donald L. Sparks

Routledge
Taylor & Francis Group

LONDON AND NEW YORK

First published 2021
by Routledge
2 Park Square, Milton Park, Abingdon, Oxon OX14 4RN

and by Routledge
52 Vanderbilt Avenue, New York, NY 10017

Routledge is an imprint of the Taylor & Francis Group, an informa business

British Library Cataloguing in Publication Data
A catalogue record for this book is available from the British Library

Library of Congress Cataloging-in-Publication Data
Names: Sparks, Donald L., author.
Title: Economic transformation in Sub-Saharan Africa : the way forward / Donald L Sparks.
Other titles: Europa introduction to ... series.
Description: Abingdon, Oxon ; New York, NY : Routledge, 2021. | Series: Europa introduction to ... series | Includes bibliographical references and index.
Identifiers: LCCN 2020049859 | ISBN 9780367498689 (hardback) | ISBN 9781003047834 (ebook)
Subjects: LCSH: Economic development–Africa, Sub-Saharan. | Africa, Sub-Saharan–Economic conditions. | Africa, Sub-Saharan–Economic integration.
Classification: LCC HC800 .S6384 2021 | DDC 338.967–dc23
LC record available at https://lccn.loc.gov/2020049859

ISBN: 978-0-367-49868-9 (hbk)
ISBN: 978-1-032-03459-1 (pbk)
ISBN: 978-1-003-04783-4 (ebk)

Typeset in Times New Roman
by Taylor & Francis Books

Contents

Tables

About the author

Donald L. Sparks, PhD, is Emeritus Professor of International Economics at the Citadel in Charleston, South Carolina, USA (where he has been named MBA Professor-of-the-Year three times) and a university lecturer in International Business at the Management Center Innsbruck, Austria.

Dr Sparks has served as a Senior Consulting Associate in the Bureau of Intelligence and Research at the US Department of State. He has been a Fulbright Professor of Economics at the University of Swaziland, now Eswatini, and at the University of Maribor, Slovenia. He was also a Fulbright Senior Specialist at the University of Swaziland. In 2013 he was a Fulbright Specialist in Economics at the African Union Commission's Department of Economic Affairs in Addis Ababa, Ethiopia. In 2019 he went to the National University of Laos as a Fulbright Specialist. He was the Department Chairman and Visiting Professor of Economics at the American University in Cairo, Egypt.

Before beginning his academic career, Dr Sparks served as the Regional Economist for Africa in the Office of Economic Analysis at the US Department of State in Washington, DC, and as a Staff Assistant to Senator Ernest F. Hollings.

Dr Sparks has published widely, including authoring the 'Economic Trends' chapter in *Africa South of the Sahara* (Routledge, annual) for each edition for the past 35 years. He has been a consultant for a number of international organizations, including the United Nations Industrial Development Organization, the United Nations Council for Namibia, the International Union for Conservation of Nature and Natural Resources, and the Economist Intelligence Unit.

He received his MA and PhD from the School of Oriental and African Studies, London, UK, and his BA from the George Washington University, USA. Dr Sparks is married to Dr Katherine Saenger and they live in Charleston, South Carolina, and Seefeld in Tyrol, Austria. They have two grown-up children and one grandson.

Foreword

African economies have suffered over many years not so much from poverty itself but from a paucity of reliable, accessible and digestible information about them. This book aims to remedy that gap. It provides an invaluable compilation of key information, statistics and facts about African economies which will be of immense use to a wide range of readers in academia, business, government and the third sector.

Compiling information about Africa is not without its controversies. It is accepted that many measures are harder to apply and reliable statistics harder to obtain in a continent where much of the economy operates on an informal basis and government statistics can conceal as much as they reveal. But we have to use what we have got, and the broad trends identified in this study are hard to deny.

As the author underlines at the outset, the COVID-19 pandemic has had a profound impact on African economies. It has in many ways underlined the importance of developing a more autonomous growth model for the continent, so that it can rely on self-generated growth, as other continents increasingly do, and not just on its trade and financial relations with the rest of the world to generate growth. This is not an argument for autarky, but for more rapid steps to develop the continent-wide economic area that African governments themselves have pledged to build.

Africa has unique advantages—a wealth of natural resources, an abundance of land and a rapidly growing young population. But it also faces some of the toughest challenges—an unyielding environment exacerbated by the effects of climate change, unequal trade relations, difficulty in accumulating and mobilizing capital, and some governments are more focused on their own survival than on the welfare of their people (though they are by no means alone in that).

But one thing African people have demonstrated in abundance is resilience. If that and their inherent entrepreneurialism can be mobilized, the prospects for the continent's future remain bright despite the current adversity. This book provides an immensely helpful guide to the basics on which Africa will build.

Dr Nicholas Westcott
Director, Royal African Society

Acknowledgements

I would like to acknowledge and thank a few of my close colleagues with whom I have had the pleasure of working over the past three decades:

Dr Adel Beshai, Department of Economics, the American University in Cairo;

Dr Steve Barnett, Management Center Innsbruck;

Dr David Konkel, Office of Economic Analysis, US Department of State;

Dr Richard Dutu, Department of Economics, Organisation for Economic Co-operation and Development.

For the past 35 years I have contributed to *Africa South of the Sahara*. I would like to acknowledge the mentoring I received from previous editors, Arthur Wayne and Katherine Murison, and editorial assistance from the current editor, Iain Frame.

Finally, this volume was greatly enhanced by the insightful comments and suggestions of Dr Patrick Ndzana, Department of Economics, the African Union Commission in Addis Ababa, to whom I give warm thanks.

Of course, any and all mistakes can be attributed to me.

Donald L. Sparks
Charleston, South Carolina

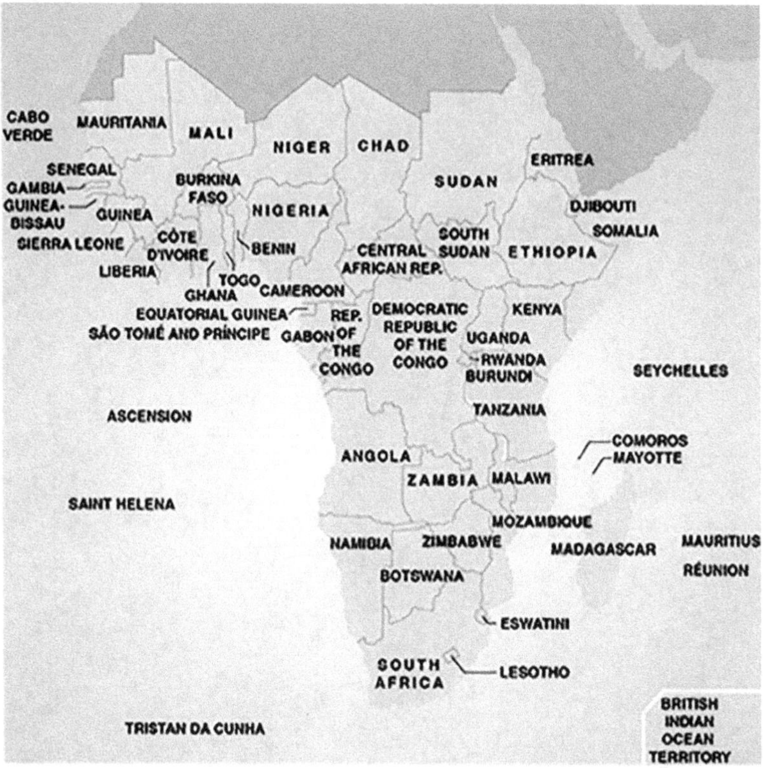
CABO VERDE
MAURITANIA
MALI
NIGER
CHAD
SENEGAL
GAMBIA
GUINEA-BISSAU
GUINEA
BURKINA FASO
NIGERIA
SUDAN
ERITREA
DJIBOUTI
SOMALIA
SIERRA LEONE
CÔTE D'IVOIRE
LIBERIA
BENIN
TOGO
GHANA
CAMEROON
CENTRAL AFRICAN REP.
SOUTH SUDAN
ETHIOPIA
EQUATORIAL GUINEA
SÃO TOMÉ AND PRÍNCIPE
GABON
REP. OF THE CONGO
DEMOCRATIC REPUBLIC OF THE CONGO
KENYA
UGANDA
RWANDA
BURUNDI
SEYCHELLES
ASCENSION
TANZANIA
COMOROS
MAYOTTE
ANGOLA
ZAMBIA
MALAWI
SAINT HELENA
MOZAMBIQUE
NAMIBIA
ZIMBABWE
MADAGASCAR
MAURITIUS
RÉUNION
BOTSWANA
ESWATINI
SOUTH AFRICA
LESOTHO
TRISTAN DA CUNHA
BRITISH INDIAN OCEAN TERRITORY

1 Introduction and recent economic developments

While coming later to sub-Saharan Africa than to many other parts of the world, the coronavirus disease (COVID-19) pandemic has hit the region with what the International Monetary Fund (IMF) has called 'an unprecedented health and economic crisis'[1]. The effects will be more severe in some countries than in others. According to the World Health Organization (WHO)'s *Situation Update* for the African region dated 2 September 2020, the number of confirmed cases for sub-Saharan Africa between 25 February and 1 September was 1,011,615, with 20,632 deaths and 829,434 recovered cases. During that period the number of cases and deaths continued a downward trend, notably in South Africa, Ghana, Kenya, Senegal and Ethiopia, countries that had been reporting the highest numbers of cases in the previous weeks. Indeed, by September South Africa, Nigeria and Ethiopia combined had accounted for 78% of the region's COVID-19 deaths. On 4 January 2021, the African CDC reported a total of 1,885,973 cases, 42,530 deaths and 1,555.915 recoveries for the region. However, because of reporting delays and poor statistical gathering in general, many experts suspect that this number undercounts the actual number of cases and deaths. It should be noted, perhaps, that the region accounts for less than 5% of confirmed cases and less than 3% of deaths reported worldwide. Only two countries, Eritrea and Seychelles have not reported any COVID-19 related deaths since the beginning of the pandemic.[2]

The IMF's latest *Regional Economic Outlook* report projected that the region's gross domestic product (GDP) for 2020 would decline by 1.6%, the lowest level on record.[3] (It should be noted that in October 2019 the IMF had projected a positive growth rate for 2020, a difference of 5.2%.) With a decline in the price of oil and other commodities, most countries will have little budgetary cushion to absorb the shock. The virus's rapid spread is likely to overwhelm the health care systems in many countries. The WHO Regional Office for Africa projected that as many as 190,000 people in Africa could die of COVID-19 and that 29m.–44m. could become infected in the first year of the pandemic if containment measures fail.

Between 1961 and 1975 the region generally experienced solid economic growth (above 5% in most cases), but this was followed by two decades of stagnation in the 1980s and 1990s.[4] Indeed, in 2000 the front cover of *The Economist* labelled Africa the 'hopeless continent'.[5] However, sub-Saharan Africa's economic output expanded at nearly twice the global rate from the dawn of the new millennium until 2015, and by 2011 *The Economist* had changed its tune and declared Africa 'the hopeful continent'.[6] However, in 2015 and 2016 economic growth slowed to its lowest levels in nearly 20 years, with the region's GDP in 'real' terms, i.e., taking inflation into account, growing by 3.3% in 2015, barely above the rate of population growth, and down from 5.0% in 2014[7]. The IMF reported that GDP increased by 3.0% in 2017, by 3.3% in 2018, by 3.1% in 2019 and, as discussed above, was forecast to decline by 1.6% in 2020, with a possible recovery of 4.1% in 2021 if the COVID-19 pandemic is successfully countered (see Table 1.1).

There were significant differences between economic growth in individual countries and regions in 2019, with some economies performing very well (led by South Sudan's GDP growth rate of 11.3%, followed by São Tomé and Príncipe, and Rwanda with 10.1%), while others experienced moderate expansion. In that year 12 other countries (Benin, Cabo Verde, Côte d'Ivoire, The Gambia, Ghana, Guinea, Kenya, Mali, Niger, Sierra Leone, Tanzania and Uganda) achieved

Table 1.1 Regional GDP growth rates (annual % change, in real terms)

	2017	*2018*	*2019*	*2020**	*2021+*
Sub-Saharan Africa (SSA)	3.0	3.3	3.1	–1.6	4.1
SSA excluding Nigeria and South Africa	4.8	4.9	4.5	0.7	4.9
Oil exporting countries	0.5	1.5	1.8	–2.8	2.6
CFA Franc Zone	4.1	4.7	4.5	1.0	5.8
ECA	5.6	6.6	5.9	2.0	5.2
ECOWAS	2.9	3.4	3.6	–1.4	3.9
SACU	1.4	1.0	0.3	–5.6	4.1
SADC	2.3	2.1	1.1	–3.4	3.9

Note: * = estimates; + = projections
Source: IMF, *Regional Economic Outlook: Sub-Saharan Africa, 2020.*

growth greater than 5%, while six countries experienced a decline (Angola, the Republic of the Congo, Equatorial Guinea, Liberia, Namibia and Zimbabwe). For 2020 the forecast is grim: economic growth is predicted to fall in every country, with Seychelles—projected to decline by 10.8%—performing the worst.

The fastest area of growth in 2019 was the East African Community (ECA, comprising Burundi, Kenya, Rwanda, South Sudan, Tanzania and Uganda) where GDP was estimated to have expanded by 5.9%, almost double the sub-Saharan region's average, but down from 4.7% in 2018. Rwanda (10.1%) recorded the highest growth rate, followed by Tanzania (6.3%), Kenya (5.9%), Uganda (4.9%) and Burundi (1.8%). However, the region is facing significant headwinds in 2020: the COVID-19 pandemic will have considerable significant effects on the region's economic output. Almost as significant, a locust outbreak regarded as the worst in a generation has spread across the East African region. Locusts can travel up to 90 miles a day and can form swarms of 80,000m. insects, with a swarm able to eat an area of crops as large as as an entire city in a day. Millions of hectares of crops have been destroyed and damages and losses could haved reached a value of US $8.500m. by the end of 2020. In the Horn of Africa more than 24m. people are food insecure and 12m. have been internally displaced, according to the World Bank, calling this a 'crisis within a crisis'.[8] The timing could not have been worse as a second wave of newly hatched locusts arrived at planting time. In addition, these plagues are very hard to control even under normal circumstances, but now the COVID-19 pandemic (with border closures and lockdowns) will make regional co-operation difficult, if not impossible

The CFA Franc Zone, comprising the Union Economique et Monétaire Ouest-Africaine—(UEMOA)—which brings together Benin, Burkina Faso, Côte d'Ivoire, Guinea-Bissau, Mali, Niger, Togo and Senegal; and the Communauté Economique et Monétaire de l'Afrique Centrale (CEMAC) which includes Cameroon, the Central African Republic (CAR), Chad, Equatorial Guinea, Gabon and Congo, grew by 4.5% in 2019, slightly down from 4.7% the year before. The fastest growing economy was Côte d'Ivoire at 6.9%. Owing to the fall in the price of petroleum, Equatorial Guinea's GDP declined by 6.1%. This region will also see its output decline in 2020, to an estimated 1.0%.

The 15-member Economic Community of West African States (ECOWAS, many of the members of which are in the Franc Zone) experienced a 3.6% growth rate in 2019, up from 3.4% in 2018. The

IMF projected that the group would record an economic decline in 2020 due principally to the pandemic.

For the 16-member Southern African Development Community (SADC), modest growth (of 1.1%) was recorded in 2019, down from 2.1% in 2018. In March 2019 Cyclone Idia—a Category 2 storm, and the strongest ever to hit the southern hemisphere—made landfall in Mozambique and travelled west into Malawi causing severe flooding and leaving more than 1,000 people dead. This was followed by another storm, Cyclone Kenneth, in April. GDP growth in these countries (as well as in Zimbabwe, which was also hard hit) for 2019 declined. In 2020 the region was projected to experience an economic contraction of 3.4%.

Unfortunately for sub-Saharan Africa, its overall positive GDP growth in recent years has not correlated with poverty reduction as had been hoped. Furthermore, the region is being confronted by daunting challenges in the near term, as discussed above. The effects of the COVID-19 pandemic will be exacerbated by slower expansion in other emerging markets, as strong growth in the region has been supported by the demand (principally for mineral commodities) from these economies. As these emerging economies (especially the People's Republic of China) continue to slow, the implications will be serious. China has become the region's major trade partner and source of foreign direct investment (FDI). In addition, tighter worldwide financial conditions could impede financial flows and FDI. Increased trade tensions between some of the world's largest economies will also have a negative impact. Worsening security conditions, especially in South Sudan, the CAR, Somalia and Nigeria, will have spillover effects on neighbouring states. Other challenges will be discussed below.

Sub-Saharan Africa has great diversities and the 49 countries of the region range significantly in terms of population, size and economic scale. Nigeria has the largest population (an estimated 215m. in 2020) and Seychelles has the smallest population, of just 98,347. The region's total population is estimated at 1,078,3m., and Africa's population is growing more rapidly than that of any other region worldwide; for many African countries the population is doubling each generation. Some 43% of the region's population is under 15 years of age. Climate and topography vary greatly and include Mediterranean, tropical and semi-tropical, desert, rainforest, savannah, mountains and plains. Some sub-Saharan countries, including South Africa, the Democratic Republic of the Congo (DRC), Botswana, Namibia and Zimbabwe, are relatively well endowed with natural resources, while others, for example Niger and Somalia, have few such assets.

Most Africans (some 60%) live in rural areas, although some countries are more intensively urbanized than others. Djibouti's urban population, for example, represents some 78% of the country's total, while in Burundi it accounts for only 13%. Generally, the region has a very low population density (50 people per sq km), which increases the cost of providing infrastructure and services. Namibia has the lowest density, with three people per sq km, and Mauritius the highest, with 623 people per sq km. GDP per head (on an international purchasing-power parity (PPP) basis) in 2018 ranged from US $1,920 in South Sudan to $30,557 in Seychelles, while the average for sub-Saharan Africa was $3,987.

Educational levels also vary greatly: nearly 100% of children in the appropriate age-group are enrolled in primary schools although the completion rate remains at only 69%, while enrolment in secondary schools averaged 43% in 2018. In that year the region's adult literacy rate was 66%, while the youth literacy rate was 79%, both representing the lowest levels of any region globally. In Benin, Burkina Faso, Chad, the CAR, Guinea, Guinea-Bissau, Liberia, Mali, Niger, Sierra Leone, Somalia and South Sudan fewer than one-half of all adult males are able to read and write. Seychelles, with an adult literacy rate of 96% ranks highest, followed by Mauritius with 91%, while the rate in South Sudan is only 35%. Expenditure on education is low, at an annual average of less than US $50 per pupil.

Life expectancy at birth for females in 2018 also varied, from 64 years in the CAR to 79 years in Seychelles, with a regional average of only 63 years, some 12 years less than the world average and more than 20 years lower than in many advanced economies. For males, the data is even worse with an average life expectancy of 59 years. In many countries, particularly in those most affected by HIV/AIDS, such as Eswatini and Botswana, average life expectancy has been reduced by more than 20 years since the mid-1980s.

The countries of the region do, however, share many common characteristics: they are, for the most part, poor and fragile. The region has been caught in a 'poverty trap' whereby low incomes lead to low savings, which lead to low investment and consumer demand; low investment results in lower productivity and lower demand leads to less revenue, both of which lead back to poverty. In 2020 sub-Saharan Africa accounted for just 3% of world trade and perhaps 1% of global GDP. The region is poor: according to the World Bank, its combined gross national income (GNI) is US $1,652,525.32m., slightly larger than that of the Spain ($1,424,230m.) In 2015, the most recent year for which data is available, some 42% of the population lived on less than $1.90 per day, the internationally recognized poverty line (see Table 1.2).

Unlike other parts of the developing world, sub-Saharan Africa had more people living in poverty in 2017 (413m.) than in 1990 (278m.), despite having reduced the percentage of people living on less than US $1.90 per day from 54% of the total population in 1990 to 41% in 2015. Just over one-half of the world's population living under the international poverty line resides in sub-Saharan Africa and it is probably home to more very poor people than in the rest of the world combined. Furthermore, sub-Saharan Africa's output per head is lower than it was 30 years earlier, having declined by about 50% in some countries. It was also the only region in which child malnutrition has not been declining in recent years.

Table 1.2 Population living on less than US $1.90 per day (2011 PPP basis, % of total population)

	1990	2008	2013	2015
East Asia and Pacific	61.4	15.2	3.7	2.3
Eastern Europe and Central Asia	1.7	3.1	2.2	1.5
Latin America and the Caribbean	16.0	7.1	4.9	3.9
Middle East and North Africa	6.2	2.7	2.3	4.2
South Asia	44.6	29.4	14.7	16.1
Sub-Saharan Africa	54.3	49.6	41.0	42.3
World	34.8	13.7	10.7	10.0

Source: World Bank, *World Development Indicators, 2020.*

Table 1.3 Population living on less than US $1.90 per day (2011 PPP basis, millions)

	1990	2017
East Asia and Pacific	984	74
Eastern Europe and Central Asia	8	10
Latin America and the Caribbean	70	30
Middle East and North Africa	14	8
South Asia	506	249
Sub-Saharan Africa	278	413
World	1,865	769

Source: World Bank, *World Development Indicators, 2019.*

Sub-Saharan Africa has the world's second most unequal distribution of income, after Latin America. None the less, the region is seeing an emerging middle class and the retail sector shows promising potential as consumer spending is expected to almost double over the next decade. Furthermore, surprising to many, there has been an increase in the number of millionaires and billionaires (measured in current US dollars). In 2020 Forbes listed 13 billionaires in sub-Saharan Africa. South Africa and Nigeria each had five billionaires, while the richest individual was Aliko Dangote of Nigeria, worth US $10,100m. In 2016 there were some 90,000 millionaires in the region, with South Africa heading the list with 40,400, followed by Nigeria with 12,300 and Kenya with 9,400. Ethiopia (with 3,100 millionaires), once thought of by many outsiders as a land of famine, has been creating millionaires at a faster rate than any other country in the region. With an economy ranked in the 10 fastest growing in the world, the number of millionaires in Ethiopia more than doubled from 1,300 in 2007 to 3,100 in 2016. However, the region has the fewest 'ultra-high net worth' individuals (whose assets amount to at least $50m.), with 894 in 2017, compared with 3,012 in Latin America, 18,138 in China, 31,938 in Europe and 74,982 in North America.

The World Bank classifies 36 countries as 'fragile and conflicted' states, with 19 in sub-Saharan Africa (see Table 1.4). These countries are 'characterized by a legacy of severe social and political turmoil, economic instability, and in some cases, violent conflict', and their economic challenges 'are often exacerbated by socio-political, governance and security problems'.

Given this vast diversity, it is, accordingly, difficult to draw general conclusions about the continent's economic performance as a whole during any given year. Additionally, the lack of current statistics for several countries makes it difficult to make accurate assessments of

Table 1.4 Countries considered to be fragile and conflict-affected

Burundi	CAR	Chad
Comoros	DRC	Congo
Côte d'Ivoire	Djibouti	Eritrea
Guinea	Guinea-Bissau	Liberia
Malawi	Mali	São Tomé and Príncipe
South Sudan	The Gambia	Togo
Zimbabwe		

Source: World Bank, *World Development Indicators, 2020.*

economic conditions. Nevertheless, some broad comparisons can be made: of the world's developing areas, sub-Saharan Africa has the worst record in virtually all of the most important social and economic indicators (see Table 1.5). The region has the lowest GNI per head, the lowest life expectancy at birth, the lowest youth literacy rate, the highest rate of adult HIV infection and the highest number of children not living past five years of age. Since 1971 the UN has viewed least developed countries (LDCs) as a category of states that are considered to be highly disadvantaged in their development process. Of the 47 LDCs listed in 2019, 33 were in sub-Saharan Africa. Of the 40 countries included within the 'low human development' category in the UN Development Programme's (UNDP) *2019 Human Development Report*, 31 were in sub-Saharan Africa (not including Somalia which was not ranked, but would be in that category), and of the 20 lowest ranked countries, 17 were from sub-Saharan Africa. Angola, Cabo Verde, Cameroon, Congo, Eswatini, Equatorial Guinea,

Table 1.5 Social and economic indicators in the developing world

	Arab States	East Asia/ Pacific	Eastern Europe/ Central Asia	Latin America/ Caribbean	South Asia	Sub-Saharan Africa
Human Development Index value (2018)	0.73	0.74	0.77	0.75	0.64	0.54
Life expectancy (years at birth, 2018)	71.9	75.3	74.2	75.4	69.7	61.2
Mean years of schooling (2018)	7.1	7.9	10.2	8.6	6.5	5.7
GDP per capita, PPP basis, (US$, 2018)	15,721	14,661	15,495	13,857	6,794	3,443
Prevalence of undernourishment, stunting (% of population under 5 years of age, 2017)	15.0	12.2	n.a.	9.6	35.0	34.1
Under-5 mortality rate (per 1,000 live births, 2018)	22	15	5	16	42	78
Youth literacy rate (% of persons aged 15–24, 2018)	90	99	100	99	89	58.7

Sources: IMF, *Regional Economic Outlook for Sub-Saharan Africa 2020*; UNDP, *Human Development Report 2019*; World Bank, *World Development Indicators, 2020*.

Ghana, Kenya, Namibia, Zambia and Zimbabwe were ranked in the 'medium human development' category, while Botswana, Gabon, Mauritius and South Africa were included within the 'high' category, and only Seychelles was ranked in the 'very high' category.

Nonetheless, despite these formidable challenges, the region may be poised at a moment of economic transformation. Domestic demand has increased in recent years and is tending to foster a larger middle class. Furthermore, demand is shifting in favour of regionally produced manufactured goods. A number of firms, including South Africa's Safaricom, M-PESA in Kenya, Nigeria's United Bank of Africa, MTM and Shopright in South Africa, and Ethiopian Airways have expanded their scope to reach a pan-African market. Start-up firms are also emerging, driving innovation which can benefit other sectors of the region's economies. With a growing young population, the region's entrepreneurial spirit can easily be enhanced. Before discussing these potential 'game changers', this study will examine some of the major trends and constraints involving the region's internal and external sectors.

Notes

1 International Monetary Fund, *Regional Economic Outlook for Sub-Saharan Africa*. April 2020.
2 https://apps.who.int/iris/bitstream/handle/10665/334127/SITREP_COVID-1 9_WHOAFRO_20200902-eng.pdf.
3 International Monetary Fund. *Regional Economic Outlook for Sub-Saharan Africa*. April 2020.
4 T. M. Callaghy and J. Ravenhill (eds), *Hemmed In: Responses to Africa's Economic Decline*. New York: Columbia University Press, 1993.
5 *The Economist*, 11 May 2000.
6 *The Economist*, 3 December 2011.
7 Unless otherwise noted, data for this survey were obtained from the World Bank's *World Economic Indicators* database (n.d.).
8 World Bank, 14 April 2020. Available at https://blogs.worldbank.org/voices/ locust-plague-fighting-crisis-within-crisis.

2 External trends

Trade, regional co-operation and south–south linkages

Sub-Saharan Africa occupies a minor role in global trade (although it is a major source of several key, strategic minerals, as will be discussed below), and accounts for less than 2% of the world's total merchandise exports (and perhaps 4% of total exports). The region generally has been importing more goods than it has been exporting, resulting in overall trade deficits. However, in 2014 imports were constrained and the overall trade balance moved into surplus (see Table 2.1) before returning to deficits in 2016 and 2017 and achieving a small surplus in 2018.

One of the most serious of the external factors Africa faces is its inability to diversify its trade. For approximately two-thirds of the countries in the region, 60% of their exports come from only one or two products. In 13 countries, one product constitutes 75% or more of total exports. For example, Angola's major export, petroleum, accounts for more than 90% of its total exports. On the other hand, South Africa's exports are the most diverse, with 39 products accounting for more than 75% of total exports, and platinum, traditionally its largest single export, accounting for only 7% of the total. In addition, the region has seen declining traditional exports and

Table 2.1 Sub-Saharan Africa's trade balance (US $'000 million at current prices)

	2014	2016	2017	2018
Exports	344.7	165.2	212.1	281.8
Imports	321.8	216.6	227.7	273.3
Trade balance	22.9	–51.4	–15.6	8.5

Source: World Bank, *World Integrated Trade Solution, 2020.*

increasing imports, both in terms of value and volume. Of total exports, raw materials continued as the most valuable export in 2018 (with 52% of the total), compared with 25% for intermediate goods. Consumer goods contributed 17% of the total, and capital goods 6% (see Table 2.2).

Most of the region's export growth has been driven by natural resources, with petroleum, ores, base metals and gold being the most important. The International Monetary Fund (IMF) has identified 20 'resource-rich' countries in sub-Saharan Africa: eight are oil exporters (Angola, Cameroon, Chad, the Republic of the Congo, Equatorial Guinea, Gabon, Nigeria, and South Sudan) and 10 non-fuel mineral exporters (Botswana, the Democratic Republic of the Congo (DRC), Guinea, Liberia, Mauritania, Namibia, Niger, Sierra Leone, South Africa and Zambia). Others have resource potential, including Mozambique, São Tomé and Príncipe, and Uganda (oil and gas) and Malawi (uranium). It should be noted that there has often been a link between resource wealth and lack of development (the so-called resource curse[1]), increased corruption and poverty. (Nigeria with vast oil and gas resources is a prime example.) Indeed, even though the resource-rich countries have recorded higher gross domestic product (GDP) growth rates since 2000, their populations as a whole have generally not benefited (they generally have lower life expectancies, extreme poverty is higher and education levels are lower). However, if resources are well managed, they can have positive effects (for example, Botswana with its diamond resources). A total of 25 countries have signed up to the Extractive Industries Transparency Initiative, which helps to ensure that earnings are shared in a more equitable and transparent manner (although the Central African Republic (CAR) has been delisted). Low commodity prices, while having recovered

Table 2.2 Composition of sub-Saharan Africa's exports and imports (US $ million, 2018)

	Exports (% of total exports)	Imports (% of total imports
Raw materials	147,933 (52%)	32,592 (12%)
Intermediate goods	69,205 (25%)	57,573 (21%)
Consumer goods	46,075 (17%)	103,532 (38%)
Capital goods	17,621 (6%)	70,851 (26%)
Total (incl. others)	280,834	264,548

Source: World Bank, *World Integrated Trade Solution, 2020.*

somewhat in 2017–18, still pose a significant challenge for the region's growth, especially as prices fell in 2019.

A generation ago, Brazil, the Russian Federation, India and the People's Republic of China accounted for perhaps 1% of African trade, with the European Union (EU), the USA and Japan commercially dominant. Since 2000 the overall growth of African exports to emerging markets (particularly China, India and Brazil) has equalled and surpassed that of shipments to developed markets (this is called South–South trade). Indeed, by 2012 exports to China, India and Brazil had exceeded those to the EU. Furthermore, China is now by far the biggest purchaser of the region's petroleum, and total trade with that country reached nearly US$37,570m. in 2018, some 14% of the total (see Table 2.3). About 70% of the region's exports to China are commodities (oil, metals and other minerals). As noted above, a sharp slowdown in China's growth, and related slackened demand, will have measurable negative effects for sub-Saharan Africa. The United Kingdom's departure from the EU (Brexit) will have serious repercussions in the region. The UK will have to make new trade agreements with sub-Saharan African countries to replace those with the EU. Although trade with the region in the past was important to the UK, in 2018 it fell to $46,000m. (about 2% of the UK's total trade). Nonetheless, South Africa is the UK's largest trade partner, with that country importing 10% of South Africa's wine exports and the UK is the second largest market for Kenya's fresh cut flowers.

The import policies of the Western industrialized countries have played a major, and often negative, role in Africa's export performance. In 2000 the Cotonou Agreement replaced successive Lomé Conventions between the EU and the group of African, Caribbean and Pacific (ACP) states. Under the new agreement, the preferential

Table 2.3 Sub-Saharan Africa's major trade partners (US $'000 million, and % share, 2018)

	Exports to	Imports from
China	37,570 (13.3%)	45,010 (16.5%)
India	26,316 (9.4%)	15,699 (5.7%)
Netherlands	4,152 (2.5%)	14,785 (5.2%)
USA	14,638 (5.2%)	13,216 (4.8%)
South Africa	12,771 (4.5%)	18,950 (6.9%)
Germany	15,929 (2.1%)	12,950 (4.7%)

Source: World Bank, *World Integrated Trade Solution*, 2020.

treatment currently in force was to be retained initially, but thereafter trade between ACP countries and the EU was to be gradually liberalized over a period of 12–15 years. A new generalized system of preferences introduced by the European Commission came into effect in 2005. The scheme offers duty-free access to the EU market for 80% of tariff lines from countries that adhere to international conventions on human rights, labour, good governance and the environment. In 2007 trade talks at the EU-Africa Summit in Lisbon, Portugal, promoted a new accord, known as the Economic Partnership Agreements (EPAs), bilateral agreements to phase out the remaining preferential trade pacts. In 2016 the Southern African Development Community (SADC) was the first regional bloc to sign an EPA (Angola has an option to join in the future) and this became fully operational in February 2018. The Economic Community of West African States (ECOWAS) and the Union Economique et Monétaire Ouest-Africaine (UEMOA) have also signed a partnership agreement. A number of other regions are currently negotiating EPAs, although some countries were resisting agreeing as they feared competition from advanced and well-established European firms and also the loss of tariff revenue. The EU has also concluded the 'Everything but Arms' agreement with many African states. Under the agreement, they are allowed to export all products, other than weapons, into the EU without having to pay tariffs. As a result, these countries do not face significant economic consequences if they choose not to join an EPA. Meanwhile, in 2004 the USA extended its Africa Growth and Opportunity Act (AGOA), although it has at various points suspended AGOA with a number of countries, including Burundi, the DRC, Eswatini, The Gambia and Rwanda, because of governance issues.

Notwithstanding the above and the benefits of these protocols, protectionism and restrictive agricultural practices (including subsidies to farmers), particularly in the EU and (to a lesser extent) the USA, have resulted in an oversupply of some agricultural commodities, and have weakened world prices. Agricultural subsidies in the USA, Japan and the EU amount to some US $360,000m. annually and eliminating these supports would benefit sub-Saharan Africa greatly. Tariff and non-tariff barriers to trade erected by the Western industrialized countries have discouraged value-added or semi-processed agricultural imports from African states. In addition to the decreased demand owing to protectionism from the developed nations, as their incomes increase, consumer demand for agricultural products does not advance proportionately. Industry is increasingly turning to substitutes, such as fibre optics for copper wires in telecommunications and beet sugar for cane sugar. As agricultural prices decline, Western consumers do not increase their consumption. Furthermore, even in countries that have dynamic export sectors such as Kenya (which exports cut flowers) and Lesotho (apparel), benefits for employment and diversification of their respective economies remain low. Finally, many African nations rely on import taxes as major sources of government revenue, and are thus hesitant to reduce such barriers.

Trade between African states is low: regional trade within sub-Saharan Africa comprises around 17% of the total (compared with Europe, where regional trade equals 68%, and Asia, where it is 59% of the total trade), according to the Brookings Institution. The current Africa Regional Integration Index 2019 reports that the continent has a low integration average score of just 0.327 out of 1. The index measures regional integration through the lens of productive, infrastructure, trade, free movement of people and macroeconomic integration. Africa is particularly 'poorly integrated on the productive and infrastructural dimensions'.[2]

None the less, recent statistics show that the combined intra-trade of the three largest regional economic communities (RECs) grew from US $30,000m. in 2004 to $102,600m. in 2014 and intra-African exports grew by 50% between 2010 and 2013, with manufacturing goods constituting nearly 40% of intra-African trade. Members of SADC have the highest proportion of intra-regional trade (around 21% of total trade is between members), with those of the Community of Sahel-Saharan States (CEN-SAD) having the least (at 4%, see Table 2.4). It should be noted that South Africa is by far the largest exporter to the region, at $14,936m. in 2018, while the next highest exporter was Nigeria with $4,653m., according to the African Export-Import Bank.

Table 2.4 Share of intra-regional trade in total trade of selected African RECs (%, 2016)

Reporting economy (# of member states)	REC members	Rest of Africa	Rest of world
SADC (15)	21.0	2.7	76.2
EAC (5)	11.5	10.1	78.4
ECOWAS (15)	10.7	5.6	83.7
COMESA (19)	7.0	9.3	83.7
CEN-SAD (28)	7.5	4.1	88.4
IGAD (8)	7.3	8.0	84.8

Source: UNCTAD, *Key Statistics and Trends in Regional Trade in Africa, 2019.*

Some two-thirds of sub-Saharan Africa's imports are finished products and its exports are dominated by natural resources with little valued added in the region. Most African states produce similar products for export, generally unprocessed primary agricultural or mineral commodities, and, as most of the value added is carried out in Western industrialized countries, there is little African demand for these products. African states themselves have often discouraged trade by their strongly inward-orientated, import-substitution development strategies, including overvalued exchange rates and protectionist trade policies. Their transport infrastructure[3] (which is often inadequate in any event) is geared towards export to the EU, Japan and North America (and more recently towards China), rather than to nearby countries. Finally, since the landlocked countries' trade has historically been principally with Europe, neighbouring countries are often viewed as competitive obstacles rather than potential markets.

African states have tried various methods of improving their trade performance, and of developing overall regional economic co-operation. Indeed, trade tariffs were reduced from 30%–40% in the early and mid-1990s to less than 15% in many countries in 2001, and to less than 10% in countries with very open economies, such as Zambia and Uganda. There have been several attempts to form free trade areas or customs unions, and the New Partnership for Africa's Development (NEPAD) has adopted regional integration as one of its core objectives.

In early 1997 the Organization of African Unity (OAU) inaugurated the African Economic Community, with the eventual goal of uniting the region's existing economic organizations into a single institution similar to the EU. The OAU was formally replaced by a new African Union (AU) in 2002. In June 2015 the AU heads of state launched the proposed African Continental Free Trade Area (AfCFTA), which, when implemented, will be the world's largest free trade area by number of countries (54). As of January 2020, 29 countries had ratified the AfCFTA and thus fulfilling the requirements for the agreement to come into effect, originally scheduled for 1 July 2020. However, because of the COVID-19 pandemic, this date has been pushed back to 2021. Once in full operation the AfCFTA will establish a market of 1,200m. people with a combined GDP of US $250,000m. The IMF believes that the agreement could be a 'game changer'. Eliminating tariffs on 90% of existing intra-regional trade flows (including North Africa) would increase trade by about 16%, according to the IMF. However, it should be noted that reducing tariffs alone is not enough to significantly boost intra-regional trade. Other impediments ('non-tariff barriers') include poor trade logistics and road infrastructure, and cumbersome border customs clearance procedures.

Africa has 14 trading blocs with overlapping members. Most countries belong to at least two blocs, and many belong to three (see Table 2.5). The Southern African Customs Union (SACU), comprising Botswana, Eswatini, Lesotho, Namibia and South Africa, is the world's oldest existing customs union—it celebrated the 100th anniversary of its foundation in 2010. It is also perhaps the most successful regional organization in sub-Saharan Africa. SACU permits free trade among its members and provides a common external tariff. Customs revenue is generally collected by South Africa and allocated to individual members according to a formula based on members' share of total trade. Such revenues are often the largest source of funding for the budgets of Eswatini, Lesotho and Namibia.

Table 2.5 Member countries of major regional economic groupings in sub-Saharan Africa

Organization	Member countries
Union Economique et Monétaire Ouest-Africaine	Benin, Burkina Faso, Côte d'Ivoire, Guinea-Bissau, Mali, Niger, Senegal and Togo
Communauté Economique et Monétaire de l'Afrique Centrale	Cameroon, CAR, Chad, Rep. of the Congo, Equatorial Guinea and Gabon
Common Market for East and Southern Africa	Burundi, Comoros, DRC, Djibouti, Eritrea, Eswatini, Ethiopia, Kenya, Madagascar, Malawi, Mauritius, Rwanda, Seychelles, Somalia, Sudan, Uganda, Zambia and Zimbabwe
East African Community	Burundi, Kenya, Rwanda, South Sudan, Tanzania and Uganda
Southern African Development Community	Angola, Botswana, Comoros, DRC, Eswatini, Lesotho, Madagascar, Malawi, Mauritius, Mozambique, Namibia, Seychelles, South Africa, Tanzania, Zambia and Zimbabwe
Southern African Customs Union	Botswana, Eswatini, Lesotho, Namibia and South Africa
Common Monetary Area (Rand Zone)	Eswatini, Lesotho, Namibia and South Africa
Intergovernmental Authority on Development	Djibouti, Ethiopia, Somalia, Eritrea, Sudan, South Sudan, Uganda

Sources: African Union, African Development Bank and UN Economic Commission for Africa, *Africa Regional Integration Report 2019*.

The two groupings which command good prospects are SADC and ECOWAS. The latter has as its eventual goal the removal of barriers to trade, employment and movement between its 15 member states, as well as the rationalization of currency and financial payments among its members. Owing to the political and economic disparity of its members, it is likely to be many years before the above objectives are fully met. SADC was established initially as the Southern African Development Co-ordination Conference (SADCC) to provide a counter, during the era of apartheid, to South Africa's economic hegemony over the region. SADCC did not initially seek an economic association or customs union, but rather to function as a subregional planning centre to rationalize development planning. Its reconstitution in 1992 as SADC placed binding obligations on member countries with the aim of promoting economic integration towards a fully developed common market. Despite SADC's desire to reduce and eventually remove trade barriers, some members have not eliminated tariffs as stipulated by the agreement, and in some cases countries that removed tariffs later reimposed them.

In 2008 three regional economic communities formed the COMESA-ECA-SADC Tripartite Free Trade Area (TFTA). The TFTA includes 26 member states with a combined population of 527m., GDP of US $624,000m. and a GDP per capita of $1,184. The three RECs make up nearly half the AU's membership of 55 countries, contribute more than 58% of the continent's GDP and account for 57% of the total population of the AU. If successful, this could encourage the formation of other FTAs in other regions of Africa.

Another important grouping, the CFA Franc Zone, was formed in 1948 and is comprises, together with France, UEMOA and the Central African Economic and Monetary Community (CEMAC) 12 former French colonies, Equatorial Guinea (a former Spanish colony) and Guinea-Bissau (a former Portuguese possession) with a total population of 155m. It operates according to four general principles: fixed parity exchange rates; convertibility guaranteed by the French Treasury; free movement of capital; and a central foreign exchange reserve. As the franc is pegged to the euro, investors from the eurozone and other countries are more likely to invest in the Franc Zone, since they are protected against exchange rate risks. Excluding France, each of the Zone's members are small states, none with a population exceeding 24m., and most are poor. A few, such as Cameroon, Congo, Equatorial Guinea and Gabon, are heavily reliant on petroleum export revenues. In May 2019 France announced that the UEOMA Franc Zone agreement was being ended (with no changes to CEMAC). ECOWAS will apparently adopt a new regional currency, the eco, which will remain pegged to the value of the euro, although there will be no requirement to keep 50% of the group's reserve with the Bank of France.

The other currency area is the Common Monetary Area, comprising Eswatini, Lesotho, Namibia and South Africa (the Rand Zone). All the members peg their currencies at par value to the South African rand. Countries in a monetary area receive benefits as well as face costs. For example, a fixed exchange rate can reduce transaction costs and ensure stability (at least in the short term). On the other hand, member countries lose control over their monetary policies, and cannot allow their currencies to devaluate individually, thus at times making their exports relatively more expensive and thus uncompetitive.

In addition to these formal trade agreements there are a number of examples of bilateral economic co-operation, mostly in regional infrastructure projects such as the Mombasa-Nairobi Corridor, the Addis Ababa to Djibouti rail connection and the Abidjan-Laos Corridor which represents some two-thirds of West African trade.

Aid, foreign debt and investment

Three of the most obvious manifestations of external difficulties are foreign debt, fluctuating levels of international aid and the problem of attracting outside investment.

Following independence most of the former colonial rulers began extending foreign economic assistance to their former colonies. The majority of British assistance, for example went (and to a large degree still goes) to Anglophone Africa, while most French assistance went to Francophone Africa. Even Germany, which lost its colonies at the end of the First World War, has provided the majority of bilateral aid to Namibia, its former colony of South West Africa. This was soon matched, and even surpassed, by the USA, Canada, the Nordic countries and Japan as well as a host of multilateral development agencies, including the United Nations Development Programme, the World Bank and the IMF. Much of this assistance was provided to counter growing (or perceived to be growing) Russian or Chinese involvement as a result of the Cold War. Both the Union of Soviet Socialist Republics and China provided funding largely for 'prestige projects' (football stadiums and railroads, for example) with a view to increasing their political influence. Initially, the bulk of this assistance was focused on large infrastructure projects such as dams or ports.

Foreign economic assistance, 'aid', can be grouped into three types: (1) humanitarian assistance for emergencies such as droughts or cyclones; (2) project aid targeted at a specific goal such as the construction of schools, roads or dams; (3) programme aid whereby donor countries provide funding to states which then decide (often with restrictions) how to use those funds.

Many countries in the region have been some of the largest recipients of international aid, which has, in many cases, been equivalent to 10%–20% of GDP, and sometimes more. Total official development assistance (ODA) to the region typically represents approximately one-third of total ODA disbursed to all developing countries.[4] The largest recipient of bilateral ODA in 2017 was Ethiopia, which received US $2,172m., although it should be noted that only Ethiopia was among the top 10 recipients worldwide of ODA in 2017 and sub-Saharan Africa accounted for just 22% of worldwide ODA. Total bilateral aid to the region was $43,583m. in 2016, the lowest total in five years, although it increased to $43,500m. in 2017 before dropping to $45,533 in 2018 (see Table 2.6).

The composition of ODA has also changed in recent years: less is now targeted at long-term economic development and a greater proportion is being devoted to short-term emergency food aid and peacekeeping activities. By 2017 the sub-Saharan region's major bilateral donors were the USA (US $11,190m.), the UK ($3,858m.), Germany ($3,691m.), France ($2,362m.) and Japan ($1,674m.). During a visit in 2014 to the AU, Chinese Premier Li Keqiang announced an aid package of $12,000m. and an increase to the China-Africa Development Fund of some $5,000m. (although no timelines were mentioned). The European Development Fund entered into force in 2015 and was endowed with €30,500m. for the period 2014–20. EU institutions provided $6,851m. in ODA in 2017, while the International Development Association contributed $6,326m.

It is a widely held view among economists that foreign aid is effective in stimulating growth in countries with sound macroeconomic environments, but that it can be unproductive and detrimental in countries with weak policy environments. For countries that are highly favoured by aid agencies and donors—the so-called donor darlings—aid

Table 2.6 Sub-Saharan Africa's net ODA receipts (US $ million)

2014	2015	2016	2017	2018
44,262	43,310	42,583	46,745	45,533

Source: OECD, *Statistics on Resource Flows to Developing Countries*, 2020.

can overwhelm their ability to put excessive donations to sensible uses that will benefit the future of their citizens. Indeed, many states have become 'aid dependent'. Sub-Saharan Africa's per head ODA totalled US $46 in 2017, the second highest among the developing world after the Middle East and North Africa (at $61 per head). In 2017–18 sub-Saharan Africa received the highest level of ODA for any region, some 23% of all ODA disbursed during the period.[5] Aid is often given for political reasons and includes construction of physical projects, such as roads and dams, with little being provided for recurrent costs. Additionally, these projects, which are funded by multiple donor agencies, are generally carried out in an uncoordinated way.

In 2010 sub-Saharan Africa's level of official (non-concessional) external debt amounted to US $278,450m., compared with $198,900m. in 2009 and $216,250m. in 2005. Nevertheless, in 2013 total external debt was equivalent to 28.5% of GDP, which compared favourably with other developing regions. The public debt-to-GDP ratio has increased, on average, by some 10 percentage points since 2014 to reach an average of 42% (and a median of 51%) of GDP in 2016. This is the highest percentage since many countries received debt relief in the 2000s under the Initiative for Heavily Indebted Poor Countries (HIPC)/Multilateral Debt Relief Initiative (MDRI). In 2018 government debt-to-GDP ratios rose to 60% in one-third of the countries in the region. According to the World Bank, the region's external short-term debt stocks stood at $68,417,864,419 in 2018.[6]

It should be noted that the composition of public debt has changed over the past few years. Countries have recently been relying on domestic bank and non-bank financing, much of it on commercial terms (with interest rates still at almost historic lows). As ODA has declined for many countries, they have turned to non-concessional sources for funding. Non-concessional debt now accounts for more than one-half of the total public debt in many countries (for example, Côte d'Ivoire, Ghana, Congo, Sudan, Zambia and Zimbabwe). Furthermore, almost one-half of the total public debt is financed in foreign currencies, making it sensitive to foreign exchange fluctuations. In addition, countries adversely affected by commodity price declines have become unable to service their debts.

The majority of the world's 'most debt-distressed countries' are in sub-Saharan Africa. Currently seven regional states are classified as being in debt distress (Congo, Mozambique, São Tomé and Príncipe, Somalia, South Sudan, Sudan and Zimbabwe). During the past two decades there has been a continuing debate on how best to reduce poor countries' debt burdens and how to fund such reductions. In

1996 the World Bank and the IMF launched the HIPC initiative to help ensure that 40 of the world's poorest countries could reduce their debts to 'sustainable levels'. The HIPC initiative was supplemented in 2005 by the MDRI, which allows for 100% relief on eligible debts by the IMF, the World Bank and the African Development Fund. The HIPC guidelines required a candidate country to complete a three-year reform programme. These reforms included economic stabilization programmes, restructuring state-owned enterprises and targeting public spending towards poverty reduction, health and education. The candidate country is then permitted a further three years to carry out additional adjustments to achieve the actual debt reductions. The region's debt service paid to official bilateral creditor nations in 2018 was US $9,400m., equivalent to about 0.5% of the region's GDP. Both the World Bank and the IMF are working on a major debt forgiveness programme in light of the COVID-19 pandemic and on 1 May 2020 announced the start of debt payment suspension for countries eligible for IDA financing. In addition, in March the World Bank created a $14,000m. fast-track facility with 25 project grants to assist 10 countries in the region.

Remittances from expatriates are also important for the region, having reached US $4,146m. in 2014. The World Bank has predicted that remittances will decline by 23% in sub-Saharan Africa in 2020 (due to the COVID-19 pandemic), although a recovery of 4% is projected in 2021. The decline is being caused by a combination of factors in key destinations where African migrants reside including in the Euro area, the USA, the Middle East and China. These large economies host a large share of sub-Saharan African migrants and are a source of nearly one-quarter of total remittances sent to the region.

Sub-Saharan Africa accounts for a modest 2% of global investment, attracting US $33,579,992,553 of foreign direct investment (FDI) in 2018.[7] Most of this is from private capital, both direct and portfolio investments. South Africa and Nigeria received approximately 65% of total FDI, which was mostly directed towards the extractive industries.

FDI can bring many benefits to developing countries, and a lack of capital can be, and has been, a major impediment to development. FDI contributes to capital formation, human capital development, technology transfer, increased managerial skills and market expansion. Generally, there is a strong correlation between higher FDI and economic growth. Since the late 1980s increased levels of FDI to developing countries have generated more intense competition for new FDI. Negotiations between host countries and potential investors generally produce an outcome more favourable to the investor, as the host country does not want to lose the deal, and often provides substantial incentives, including tax holidays or lower taxes, direct subsidies and other arrangements (sometimes referred to as a 'race to the bottom'). In any event, until very recently sub-Saharan Africa had a poor record of attracting such investment (and it still only receives 5% of worldwide FDI), although FDI flows to sub-Saharan Africa climbed by 13% in 2018 to US $32,000m., recovering ground after successive contractions in the two previous years.[8] According to the World Bank, the top countries for FDI inflows in 2019 were South Africa ($4,624,502,000); Nigeria ($3,299,085,000); Congo ($3,366,085,000); Ethiopia ($2,516,228,000); Ghana ($2,318,800,000); and Mozambique ($2,180,768,000). The total FDI for the region in 2019 was $29,199,715,000.[9]

Traditionally, over one-half of FDI to the region has come from the UK (the largest single investor), France, the Netherlands, South Africa and the USA. However, in recent years China has become a major investor: China's FDI has surged from US $75m. in 2003 to $5,400m. in 2018 and most of that investment has been in the oil producing states of Nigeria and Sudan, or in South Africa and Zambia. In 2015 the largest investors were the USA ($6,400m.), the UK ($5,800m.), France ($5,400m.) and China ($3,500m.), while investment from South Africa totalled $2,220m.

While foreign investors are attracted by the region's vast raw materials, potential high returns and low-wage economies, they are fearful of internal political volatility and the uncertainty of securing the enforcement of commercial contracts. These considerations, combined with the deteriorating human and physical infrastructure, have virtually extinguished investor confidence. Investor perception is of major importance. Investors appear more confident about improvements in tariffs, the rule of law and access to financing. Increased investment in recent years has arisen partly because governments have worked hard to make life easier for investors.

A further major problem is that African capital flight is huge.[10] An estimated US $1,200,000m. of illicit financial flows left the region between 1980 and 2009, roughly equivalent to the region's current economic output. Such flows are generated from tax evasion, bribes, money laundering and transactions from cross-border smuggling. Added to this capital flight is a large 'brain drain' of skilled human resources due to the lack of suitable jobs at home (or to a variety of other reasons, including personal security). Sub-Saharan African countries that invest in training doctors have ended up losing some $2,000m., as those doctors leave home to find work abroad.

Significantly, the attraction of the industrial countries is likely to grow. Health care is but one illustration of the severe problems caused when the very skilled people trained and needed to develop a country leave for better opportunities. On the positive side, however, there are signs of increasing numbers of professional Africans returning home (a 'reverse brain drain'). Finally, an African Development Bank report estimated that Africans hold as much as 40% of their financial portfolios outside Africa. If these funds returned, the region would increase its capital stock by about two-thirds.[11]

Local equity markets remain small in the region, and the majority of exchanges list only a handful of stocks. The region's largest exchange (and the 19th largest in the world by market capitalization) in Johannesburg, South Africa, listed 472 companies in 2017. Market capitalization totalled US $1,007,000m. in that year, up from $182,000m. in 2003. Much of the stock in the region is owned by non-Africans. For example, more than half of the top 40 companies listed on the Johannesburg stock exchange are owned by foreigners.[12] Private portfolio flows into the region are much smaller than FDI flows, and South Africa is the principal destination, accounting for some 80% of the total. Mauritius is the most active portfolio investor in intra-African portfolio investments.

During the past few years several countries—South Africa, Seychelles, Congo, Côte d'Ivoire, Ghana, Gabon, Kenya, Senegal, Nigeria, Namibia, Zambia, Tanzania, Rwanda and Mozambique—have issued sovereign bonds (also known as Eurobonds, although a few countries are denominating these bonds in local currencies). In 2006 Seychelles became the first country in sub-Saharan Africa (other than South Africa) to issue such bonds. One year later Ghana issued US $750m. worth of bonds and since then others have followed. Indeed, in 2014 Zambia issued a $1,000m. bond to help to finance its deficit. Kenya's record offering of $2,000m. in that year was oversubscribed fourfold. In 2017 sovereign bond issuances soared to $4,600m. compared to $750m. in 2016. Sovereign borrowing accounted for 70% of total non-concessional borrowing in 2016. These bonds are attractive because their yields are much higher (because of the risk) than those found in the safer, more traditional markets of the advanced economies. However, the potential negative to this trend is that should the economies stall, the countries will be hard pressed to service the bonds, especially given the budgetary constraints posed by the COVID-19 pandemic.

Notes

1 G. M. Khadiagala,'Global and Regional Mechanisms for Governing the Resource Curse in Africa', *Politikonj: South Africa Journal of Political Studies*, 42(1), 2015.
2 African Union, African Development Bank, UN Economic Commission for Africa, *Africa Regional Integration Report 2019*.
3 T. Corrigan, 'Rethinking Infrastructure in Africa: A Governance Approach', *Occasional Paper* 252. Johannesburg: South African Institute of International Affairs, 2017.
4 W. Easterly, *The White Man's Burden: Why the West's Efforts to Aid the Rest Have Done So Much Ill and So Little Good*. Oxford: Oxford University Press, 2007; and D. Moyo, *Dead Aid: Why Aid Is Not Working and How There Is Another Way for Africa*. London: Penguin, 2010.
5 Organisation for Economic Co-operation and Development, *Development Aid at a Glance*. Paris: OECD, 2019. Available at www.oecd.org/developm ent/aid-for-trade-at-a-glance-22234411.htm.
6 World Bank, *International Debt Statistics*. Washington, DC: World Bank, 2020.
7 www.africaoutlookmag.com/industry-insights/article/1162-analysing-the-la test-african-fdi-figures-from-unctad.
8 UNCTAD, *World Investment Report*, June 2019.
9 World Bank, *World Development Indicators*. Available at https://datacata log.worldbank.org/dataset/world-development-indicators.
10 L. Ndikumama and J. K. Boyce, 'Rich Presidents of Poor Nations: Capital Flight from Resource-Rich Countries in Africa', *ACAS Bulletin*, 87, 2012.
11 African Development Bank, *Illicit Financial Flows and the Problem of Net Resource Transfers from Africa: 1980–2009*. Abidjan: AfDB, 2012.
12 Alex Hogg, 'Foreign Shareholders Now Control Almost Half of the JSE's Top 40 Companies", *Biz News*, December 2015.

3   Internal trends

Africa also faces a number of 'internal' economic problems, which, in the view of many analysts, may outweigh the 'external' factors discussed earlier in this volume. Many countries in sub-Saharan Africa are still suffering from a crisis of statehood and a crisis of capability.[1] An urgent priority is to rebuild state effectiveness through an overhaul of public institutions, the resurrection of the rule of law, and credible checks on the abuse of state power. Indeed, as far back as 1989 a World Bank study on sub-Saharan Africa's quest for sustainable growth suggested that 'underlying the litany of Africa's problems is "a crisis of governance"'.[2] This, unfortunately, is still the case in all too many countries.

Governance, parastatal organizations, the business environment and the informal sector

After independence in the 1950s and 1960s, most newly formed African governments believed they had three fundamental choices for developing their economies and for encouraging industrialization in the broadest sense. They could: (i) nationalize existing entities; (ii) seek to attract private investment from abroad by offering favourable investment incentives (tax 'holidays', for example); or (iii) invest heavily in public enterprises. Most governments adopted combinations of all three, but virtually every national administration south of the Sahara opted for an import substitution strategy and substantial parastatal involvement. By and large, at independence, there was little indigenous involvement in the modern sector, and almost none in the industrial sphere. Unfortunately, there were few successful attempts to link the large state-owned enterprises (SOEs or parastatals) into the wider economy. In addition, these SOEs were often protected by tariffs and other barriers to foreign competition, and thus had little incentive to become efficient.

Most of the early parastatal organizations operated in natural monopoly areas: large infrastructural projects (highways, railways and dams) and social service facilities (schools, hospitals and medical clinics). Government soon moved into areas that had previously been dominated by the private sector (or, at least, traditionally dominated by the colonial sector in most 'mixed' economies), and parastatal bodies accounted for more than one-third of employment in many countries. Indeed, by the 1980s the majority of wage earners in the formal sector were state employees. In many countries, well over one-half of the national budget was devoted to state salaries. Jobs in the SOEs often were offered to politically connected persons without regard to qualifications. Most analysts have generally considered parastatal organizations to have failed, at least in terms of economic efficiency criteria. After independence, most African countries expanded the size of their civil service more rapidly than their economic growth justified. This expansion was designed to provide employment, but civil servants received lower and lower real wages, and many governments became bloated and corrupt.

For most states the need for better governance became critical and many governments have scaled back the role of parastatals in recent years. Related to better governance is fiscal discipline: putting government debt on a sustainable track. In many cases government revenue projections are overly optimistic and spending levels unrealistic. The result has too often been large and unstainable budget deficits. Recent reforms have helped but the African Development Bank (AfDB) lists several remaining challenges: weak tax and customs administrations; lack of transparency; low taxpayer morale; and hard to tax sectors (for example, the informal sector, see below).

The general perception is that the region has not developed an appropriate enabling environment for the private sector to grow and flourish. Indeed, it lags behind other regions in providing a quality business environment, although that is changing. The World Bank's 2020 *Doing Business* [3] report cited a record number of reforms (107), making it easier to do business. The average time to register a business has declined from 59 days in 2006 to 23 days in 2020. However, compared to the previous year, sub-Saharan African economies raised their average ease of doing business score by just 1 percentage point. Mauritius was ranked 13th on the Bank's list of the easiest places to do business, just ahead of Australia, while Rwanda (at 38th place) was the next highest placed African country. Indeed, Rwanda, which 25 years ago suffered from genocide, is now considered friendlier to investors than the Netherlands. None the less, of the 40 countries (out of a total of 190) that ranked as the hardest in which to conduct business, 22 were in sub-Saharan Africa.

The World Economic Forum[4] ranked sub-Saharan Africa as the world's least competitive region. Mauritius was ranked as the most competitive country in the region (52nd out of 141 countries worldwide). Of the 30 countries ranked at the bottom of the list, 28 were from sub-Saharan Africa. South Africa, the second most competitive in the region, moved to the 60th position, while Namibia (94th), Rwanda (100th), Uganda (115th) and Guinea (122nd) made significant improvements. Kenya (95th) and Nigeria (116th) also improved their performances. It should be noted, perhaps, that of the 25 countries that have improved their health pillar score by two points or more, 14 are from sub-Saharan Africa, making strides to close the gaps in longer life expectancy.

Registering property is difficult and costly (although as noted above it is becoming faster), and in addition to the delays owing to excessive bureaucracy, there are often further delays caused by poor infrastructure, as discussed below. Many countries in the region also ranked poorly in Transparency International's Corruption Perceptions Index; in 2019 only three countries—Seychelles (27th), Botswana (34th) and Cabo Verde (41st) ranked in the top 50 least corrupt countries worldwide.[5]

The informal sector accounts for nearly 90% of non-agricultural employment and accounts or 40% of official GDP. Many small firms see no advantage in joining the formal sector. For example, formal employment usually entails taxation and rigid employment contracts making the recruitment and dismissal of employees difficult. Productivity is typically much less than in the formal sector (at approximately 14% on average). The majority of workers in the informal sector lack income security and employment benefits, while life expectancy is lower and poverty higher than for those working in the formal sector. Most informal sector workers (and their families) will not have had adequate access to health care during the COVID-10 pandemic.

Many business owners have poor proof of title, and without adequate property rights and contract enforcement, lenders are hesitant to extend credit. While the types of activities carried out in the informal sector existed prior to colonialism, independence brought in the distinction between informal and formal activities, as countries around the region sought to formalize or 'modernize' their economies. The focus then (and indeed to some degree today) was rapid industrialization. Although the informal sector has declined in a few countries (e.g.

Botswana, Ethiopia, Malawi, Rwanda and Tanzania), for much of the region it is the informal sector, not the formal sector that is the growth engine. Thus, how governments treat the informal sector has a profound impact on employment, growth, equity and sustainability.

Civil strife

Social and political stability are generally associated with higher economic growth rates. Since independence, more than one-half of sub-Saharan African countries at one time or another have been caught up in civil wars, uprisings, mass migrations and/or famine. It has been suggested that typically civil wars in the region last about seven years and cause GDP to decline by more than 2% for each year of strife. Furthermore, it typically takes a country about 14 years after the end of the conflict to recover to its pre-war growth levels. Many post-conflict governments continue to spend heavily on their military, thus reducing the potential peace dividend. Conflicts can be both a cause and consequence of poverty and some observers have termed this the 'conflict trap'. The Office of the United Nations High Commissioner for Refugees (UNHCR) estimated that in 2015 sub-Saharan Africa hosted more than 26% of the world's refugee population.[6] It also estimated that the region hosted about one-half of the world's total internally displaced people. In 2019 there were approximately 18m. displaced persons in the region.

Although the intensity of conflict is now lower than during the 1990s, strife continues to plague many areas of the region, with conflicts sometimes involving neighbouring countries and thus inhibiting economic growth for the entire sub-region. Conflict tends to reduce the tax base while at the same time increasing government expenditure, to the detriment of much-needed social services. Moreover, 'traditional' wars have been replaced by non-state-based conflicts. The militant Islamist group Boko Haram has continued its activities in Nigeria, Cameroon, Chad and Niger, although at a lower level than a few years ago. Conflicts in Somalia and Sudan have caused a high number of battle-related deaths, while violence in Mali, the Central African Republic (CAR) and South Sudan may have resulted in over 1,000 casualties annually in each country.

Health, population and education

Life expectancy in the region is 61 years and falls well below the 80 years in the advanced economies. Perhaps the leading factor causing this is inadequate heath care: virtually all African states face significant problems in providing health services, and the region spends 5.1% of its GDP on health services (compared to a world average of 10.2%). This expenditure has been unevenly distributed among countries: for example, in 2016 Angola spent 2.8% of its GDP on health, while Sierra Leone spent 15.5%. Moreover, care was unevenly distributed throughout many countries, with most health facilities concentrated in urban areas. In 2016 Seychelles led the region with one physician per 1,000 people, compared with the region's average of 0.3. The COVID-19 pandemic is dramatically illustrating the lack of health care infrastructure. For example, ventilators are essential in treating COVID-19 patients, but South Sudan (with a population of 11m.) has four ventilators, the CAR (with a population of 5m.) only three. According to the World Health Organization (WHO), there are some 2,000 working ventilators in the region (compared to more than 170,000 in the USA). WHO also noted the shortage of intensive care hospital beds in sub-Saharan Africa, which had an estimated five beds per 1m. people, compared to about 4,000 beds per 1m. in Europe.

Less than one-third of the region's population has access to adequate sanitation, and in some nations this is as low as 8%–15%. Proper hygiene is one of the most effective ways to prevent the spread of disease, and this has become more evident during the COVID-19 pandemic. The UN's Sustainable Development Goals are monitoring the percentage of people who have facilities to wash their hands at home with soap and water and recent related studies indicate that access to water and soap for handwashing varies immensely in the 70 countries for which data is available, from 15% of the population in some countries in sub-Saharan Africa to 76% in western Asia and northern Africa. In 2015 68% of the total sub-Saharan African population had access to clean water (compared to 47% in 1990), and among the urban population the figure is 87%. Significantly, some 80% of illness in Africa's least developed countries can be associated with inadequate water supplies or poor sanitation. Indeed, every day, about 500 children in sub-Saharan Africa die due to diarrhoeal diseases. Urban sanitation access ranges from a high of 89% of the population in Angola's cities, to 20% in Ghana, with the region's average at 30% (up from 24% in 1990).

HIV/AIDS is a major public health and economic development concern and cause of death in many parts of sub-Saharan Africa. Although the continent is home to only about 15% of the world's population, sub-Saharan Africans accounted for an estimated 70% of all people living with HIV and 70% of all AIDS deaths in 2011, and by 2012 some 70% of new infections. Indeed, by 2013 of the 1.5m. AIDS-related deaths worldwide, 1.2m. were in sub-Saharan Africa. The majority of HIV/AIDS cases are concentrated in Eastern and Southern Africa (where some 20m. people are infected), while Central and Western Africa have about 5m. cases (see Table 3.1). In 2018 there were 37.9m. people living with HIV globally.

HIV/AIDS, malaria and deaths from conflicts have contributed to a decline in life expectancy in several states, particularly those hardest hit in southern Africa. Indeed, the region saw a dramatic drop in life expectancy around 1990, which coincided with the rise in HIV-AIDS. In Botswana, life expectancy fell by a decade and in Eswatini it fell by two decades. However, since the early 2000s, as progress has been made on tackling HIV, life expectancy has been rising again, but it is only now approaching levels prior to the HIV pandemic. While the pandemic has slowed dramatically in the region (the death rate fell by 39% between 2005 and 2013), HIV/AIDS remains a threatening health problem in many countries, and more than 20m. Africans have died from the disease.

AIDS in Africa generally affects young adults (aged 20–45 years) in their most economically productive years, and in Africa the educated, urban elite have been hardest hit. In response, a number of initiatives have been launched to educate the public about HIV/AIDS, such as the 'abstinence, be faithful, use a condom' campaign. The number of HIV-positive people in Africa receiving anti-retroviral therapy (ART) rose from 1m. to 7.1m. between 2005 and 2012. By 2016 some 54% of all people living with HIV/AIDS were getting some treatment, although 67% of men and 57% of women were not receiving ART, and in Nigeria, Africa's most populous country, 70% of the people do not have access to treatment. By the end of 2017 15.3m. people living with HIV in the region had access to life-saving antiretroviral drugs (ARVs), representing 70% of the 21.7m. people accessing ARVs globally, according to WHO.[7] In Eastern and Southern Africa, over 905 of pregnant women have access to ARVs, while in Central and Western Africa only about 60% do (see Table 3.1).

The International Partnership Against AIDS in Africa was launched in 1999, with the participation of African governments, the UN, international donors, and the private and community sectors. The Partnership has campaigned for, and 10 states have received, access to lower-cost generic drugs to fight HIV/AIDS and South Africa has successfully negotiated agreements with pharmaceutical companies to produce drugs domestically. In 2000 the USA agreed to allow African states to develop generic AIDS vaccines without regard to US patent protections and the drastic fall in prices mentioned above has subsequently enabled treatment expansion.

Approximately 11% of disease-induced deaths in Africa are caused by malaria. The region accounts for 93% of malaria cases and 94% of the 405,000 malaria deaths annually (mostly children) worldwide. (The Republic of the Congo and Nigeria account for two-fifths of those malaria deaths.) Unfortunately, the number of malaria cases increased by 5m. in 2016, and malaria's toll is greater than that of all other tropical diseases combined. A child dies every minute from malaria in sub-Saharan Africa. Some researchers believe that had malaria been eradicated 30 years ago, the region's GDP would now be one-third higher than it is, and the World Bank estimates that malaria takes US $12,000m. of Africa's GDP every year.

African trypanosomiasis (sleeping sickness), which had been virtually eradicated in the early 1960s, reappeared in 1970 and is now widespread, occurring in 36 sub-Saharan African countries. Owing to a lack of screening and treatment, and regional conflict, this disease has become the greatest cause of mortality in areas of South Sudan, Angola and the Democratic Republic of Congo (DRC). None the less, there have been some successful attempts to combat disease in the region. For example, onchocerciasis (river blindness) has been virtually eliminated in West Africa; WHO estimated that its programme for the control of the disease (concluded in 2002) prevented 600,000 new cases and only 977 cases were recorded in 2018.

Table 3.1 Regional HIV-AIDS treatment coverage (2018)

	% of pregnant women accessing ARVs	*% of adults (aged 15 and over) living with HIV accessing ARVs*	*% of children (aged 0–14 years) living with HIV accessing ARVs*	*% of all people living with HIV accessing ARVs*	*Number of people living with HIV (million)*
East and Southern Africa	92%	67%	62%	67%	20.6
West and Central Africa	59%	54%	28%	51%	5.0

Source: UNAIDS, *Fact Sheet: World AIDS Day 2019.*

African countries have some of the highest annual average population growth rates in the world, with a regional average of 2.7% in 2018: Angola, Burundi, Chad, the DRC, Equatorial Guinea, Mali, Niger, Tanzania, and Uganda all had population growth rates of 3.0% or greater. Most of sub-Saharan Africa is undergoing a demographic transition, owing to declining infant mortality and fertility rates. Sub-Saharan Africa's population, about 1,107m. in 2019, is projected to rise to 2,000m. by 2050 and to 3,700m. by 2100. By 2035 the number of sub-Saharan Africans reaching working age (15–64 years) will exceed that of the rest of the world combined. Sub-Saharan Africa's share of the global labour force is thus projected to increase from 10% in 2010 to 37% by 2100. Indeed, the region will need to create jobs at an extraordinary rate, about 18m. per year until 2035, in order to absorb the growing labour force. While the demographic transition may ensure the labour supply side of growth, a more diversified and robust economy means that labour demand is needed to turn the transition into a 'demographic dividend'. Many parts of Africa could enjoy the benefits of the 'youth bulge' (as happened in many countries in East and South Asia). However, failure to seize the opportunity is likely to result in even greater numbers of unemployed people along with increasingly negative social and economic consequences.

The demographic changes are projected to vary across sub-Saharan Africa. The biggest increase in population will occur in the eastern and western areas, while population growth will remain largely flat in the southern subregion, reflecting the demographic transitions of its largest economy, South Africa. Nigeria is expected to have the largest increase in population. As the African population grows in size, it will also alter in shape: the median age now is 20 years, compared with 30 years in Asia and 40 years in Europe. Africa's dependency ratio (the ratio of working-age population to dependants) is close to 1:1, compared with East Asia's ratio of 2:1.

Most African countries have family planning programmes, and some have set targets for population growth. Stemming rapid population growth in Africa is difficult because of social as well as economic factors. Most Africans live in rural areas on farms and require large numbers of helpers. The cheapest way of obtaining such assistance is for a farmer to have more children. Owing to the high infant mortality rate (resulting from poor health and nutrition), rural couples tend to want, and have, more babies. Additionally, most African countries do not have organized old-age support schemes, and children are often viewed as potential providers of support for the elderly. However, Africa now seems to be on the path towards smaller families that has occurred in much of the world, although at a very slow rate. One important success is the recent huge decline in child mortality. A recent World Bank study shows that in 16 of the 20 countries for which data is available, child mortality rates (the number of deaths of children under five per 1,000 live births) have fallen since 2005. Twelve countries demonstrated falls of over 4.4% per year, higher than in China during the early 1980s. Indeed, the rates of decline in African child mortality are the highest in the world in the past 30 years. None the less, while the under five years old mortality rate of 180 per 1,000 live births in 1990 declined to 78 in 2016, this is still the world's highest and remains almost double the world average.

There has been a direct link between education and growth— between 1960 and 1980 the African countries that had higher percentages of children enrolled in primary school also had higher economic growth rates. Low primary school enrolment hampers economic development. The percentage of malnourished children rose from 31% in 1992 to 35% in 2015, the only region in the world to witness such an increase: children who do not have enough to eat perform poorly in school. A further key factor is that of increased education for women, which is clearly associated with lower fertility rates. A recent study by the World Bank found that the three countries with declining fertility—Botswana, Kenya and Zimbabwe—had the highest levels of female schooling and the lowest rates of child mortality. The study also indicated that in the Sahel, where female schooling rates are lowest, both fertility rates and child mortality have remained high.

Shortly after independence, most countries in the sub-Saharan region initiated programmes aimed at establishing universal primary education. Currently, nearly 100% of children in the appropriate age-group are enrolled in primary schools (compared with 79% in 1999, and some 69% of these complete primary school), while 43% are enrolled in secondary school. Only 30% of each class graduate from junior secondary school, while even fewer (12%) graduate from senior secondary school. Access to tertiary education, while increasing in recent years, still remains the lowest in the world, with only 9% of the relevant aged population enrolled in 2018. Furthermore, while the gender gap in education has narrowed (especially in primary schools) in many countries, there are areas where fewer than three girls are enrolled in secondary education for every four boys.

Rapid urbanization has also imposed stresses on many African economies. Africa is still predominantly rural and agricultural. In 1980 about 75% of the region's population lived in rural areas, but that figure has declined to around 60%. However, approximately 70% of Africa's poorest people live in rural areas. Urbanization has increased at an alarming pace (it is currently growing at an annual rate of 4%, the highest in the world), and it has been forecast that by 2025 Africa's urban population will be three times larger than in 2000, with more than one-half of the population living in cities. More than 45% of all urban-dwelling sub-Saharan Africans reside in cities with more than 500,000 inhabitants, compared with only 8% in 1960, when there were only two cities in the region with populations exceeding 500,000. Unemployment and underemployment are rampant in every major city of Africa and living conditions in virtually every city have worsened over the last two decades. In addition, the cost of living is relatively more expensive in Africa than in many other developing regions.

Until relatively recently most African governments did not regard rapid population growth or environmental degradation as matters for concern. Indeed, until fairly recently most areas of the region practised what is known as 'slash and burn' agriculture, a technique that can only succeed where land is abundant. During the past decade a succession of countries, realizing that their resources cannot service their population growth, have begun to recognize the necessity for environmental protection.

The natural environment and climate change

Africa's environment has been under intense pressure, especially during the past 20 years. With the increases in population discussed above, overcultivation and overgrazing have turned vast areas into virtual wastelands. Also, wood is collected for heating and cooking, supplying 70% of domestic energy needs. During 1990–2005 sub-Saharan Africa recorded the highest annual average rate of deforestation in the world. During 1990–2007 forest area as a percentage of total land area declined from 29.4% to 26.2%. The Food and Agriculture Organization of the UN estimates that old growth forests in the region are being cut down at more than 4m. ha per year, twice the world's deforestation average. According to the World Bank, African forests are believed to contain 45% of the world's biodiversity, while forest-related activities account for at least 10% of GDP for 17 nations in the region. In addition, the region contains about 15% of the world's remaining forests, second to South America in the amount of tropical forests that are the most effective in removing carbon from the air. Across the Sahel population increases and changes in settlement patterns are putting pressure on fragile ecosystems. Fertile land is turning into dust, as people living in the transitional zone between the Sahel and the Sahara cut down trees for charcoal and send their animals further out in search of pasture. Civil wars have also contributed significantly to environmental degradation.

It is predicted that climate change will affect Africa more seriously than any other area in the world, although the region produces only about 7% of the world's greenhouse gases. Greater rainfall variability will contribute to more flooding and droughts, and will exacerbate the malaria problem. Smallholders, already often in danger, will be placed at even greater risk. In 2007 the UN's Intergovernmental Panel on Climate Change predicted a minimum increase in temperature of 2.5° C by 2030, suggesting that food security will be severely compromised. The *Africa Adaptation Gap* report published by the UN Environment Programme in 2015 warned that climate change could reduce crop output by as much as 20% by 2070, while sea level rises would have dire economic consequences. For example, the projected 70 cm sea level rise by 2070 could devastate the city of Dar es Salaam (Tanzania), East Africa's major port. It should be noted, however, that climate change could bring benefits; for example, Eastern Africa could see increased rainfall in its parched highland areas. In addition, as noted above, Cyclone Idia was the strongest storm ever to hit the southern hemisphere where it made landfall in Mozambique and travelled west causing severe flooding, affecting more than 2.6m. people and leaving more than 1,000 deaths in its wake. This was followed by another devastating storm, Cyclone Kenneth, in 2019.

Many government leaders have suggested in the past that the achievement of economic growth is inconsistent with environmental protection, and that African development can only advance at the expense of its environment. It has only been in recent years that the two goals have been recognized as not mutually exclusive. Indeed, it is now generally accepted that sustained economic growth is impossible without adequate environmental protection. Specifically, many countries, such as Kenya, Tanzania and South Africa, increasingly depend on tourism based on wildlife and undisturbed natural habitats. However, no country in the region ranked highly on the 2019 Travel and Tourism Competitiveness Index: Mauritius was the highest ranking country, with a global ranking of 54th, followed by South Africa at 61st position and Seychelles at 62nd. Of the 140 countries ranked, 19 of the bottom 20 are from sub-Saharan Africa. While attracting only 6% of the world's tourists, the region has the potential for significant growth (in fact the World Tourism and Travel Council—WTTC— estimated a 4.4% increase in tourism's contribution to GDP in 2017).

Table 3.2 International tourism in Sub-Saharan Africa

	2009	2018
Inbound tourists ('000)	28,335	47,630
Inbound tourism expenditure (US $ million)	24,022	35,667

Source: World Bank, *World Development Indicators 2020.*

The number of visitors and their related expenditure has increased considerably since 2009 (see Table 3.2). In 2018 sub-Saharan Africa attracted 47m. visitors, compared with 6.7m. visitors in 1990, and its receipts from tourism for the same year amounted to more than US $35,000m., or 2.8% of the region's GDP. According to the WTTC, the direct contribution of travel and tourism to GDP was $40,100m. (2.6% of total GDP) in 2016, and was forecast to increase to $66,900m. (2.7% of total GDP) by 2027. However, as a result of the COVID-19 pandemic, these estimates have been significantly revised downward. It is unclear when the economic damage to the tourism sector will be repaired, but the sector is not likely be return to its 2019 levels until 2022 at the earliest.

Physical infrastructure, the structure of the economies and employment

For most countries in the region physical infrastructure—including transportation, electricity and communications—has generally deteriorated since the achievement of independence in the early and mid-1960s. With 16 landlocked countries, high transportation costs have hampered growth. Additionally, essential services such as electric power, water, roads, railways, ports and communications have been neglected, particularly in rural areas. Indeed, the region's energy infrastructure is tiny and fragile, and service is unpredictable. The region has what the World Bank has branded an 'infrastructure deficit'. There have been some recent positive developments: the region is now spending almost US $7,000m. on road paving and the 4,500-km Trans-Sahara Highway (linking Lagos north to Algiers) is currently 85% paved (the rest is sand). Major rail projects (generally financed by China) are being completed, including a recent link between Angola, Zambia and the DRC, and a new electric rail line between Addis Ababa (Ethiopia) and Djibouti was opened, while a light rail system was brought into operation in the Ethiopian capital in 2015. Currently, about 20% of the World Bank's lending is focused on transport projects and in 2014 it launched a Global Infrastructure Fund. The

European Union (EU) has financed an African Infrastructure Fund since 2007.

An integrated and well-maintained road system is vital for a country's economic growth and development. The region has approximately 1,052,000 km of classified road network, another 492,000 km of unclassified roads and about 193,000 km of urban roads for a total of 1.75m. km (according to the World Bank), making them some of the most valuable state assets. However, in spite of their importance, roads have been badly managed and over one-half of the roads in sub-Saharan Africa are in very poor condition; in many countries the road network is woefully inadequate. In the DRC, for example, it has fewer miles of paved roads than Luxembourg, although the DRC is four times the size of France. Even in countries where the road network is good, for example in South Africa, recent budgetary constraints have delayed much-needed maintenance and expansion. Poor transportation affects all facets of African life, from commerce to health care to schooling. Some 70% of Africa's rural population lives more than one mile from an all-season road. Poor roads add to the costs of production in a region with the world's highest poverty rates. The costs of transporting goods in Africa are the highest in the world. For example, for three Francophone countries (Cameroon, Côte d'Ivoire and Mali) road transport costs are 40% more expensive than in France (where labour costs are much higher than in Africa). Poor road conditions can increase fuel consumption and the need for vehicle maintenance due to damage and reduce the life of tyres and of vehicles. Owing to lower speeds, vehicles are not as efficient as they could be.

Higher transportation expenses raise the costs of doing business, impede private investment and add another barrier to Africa's ability to take advantage of the rapid growth in world trade. Trade is highly sensitive to transport costs: a 10% decrease in such costs could increase Africa's trade by 25%. Of all the world's regions, intra-regional trade is lowest in sub-Saharan Africa. While there are many reasons for this (e.g. tariff and non-tariff barriers, cumbersome customs procedures, lack of product diversification, the similarity in production among neighbouring countries), poor roads play a major role. For many areas it is a lack of sufficient maintenance rather than a lack of infrastructure itself that hinders business growth and, even where the infrastructure exists, it is often of poor quality. The cost of exporting or importing a standard cargo container of goods costs about US $2,000, or twice the amount in other regions of the world. The World Bank estimated that the region requires $22,000m. annually for both capital and maintenance expenditures. To address these problems, regional leaders and their private sector counterparts met in Dakar, Senegal, in June 2014 to agree on how to finance 16 regional infrastructure projects they considered as priorities. The Dakar Agenda for Action appealed for a public-private partnership to work with the AfDB to find innovative ways for funding.

Sub-Saharan Africa has been confronted by a number of serious energy challenges, mainly related to insufficient generation capacity and an over-reliance on fossil fuels. Due to the region's small, fragmented energy markets, electrical supply systems cannot take advantage of economies of scale, and electricity is therefore expensive (although often heavily subsidized). Excluding South Africa, the region's entire electric generation capacity (63 GW) is comparable to that of Spain. About one-quarter of the population has access to electricity, compared with 40% in low-income economies elsewhere. The region has the world's lowest per capita consumption of electricity at 480 kWh (in 2014), compared to a world average of 3,125 kWh. The region uses only 3% of its renewable water for electricity generation, compared with 52% in South Asia. In addition, climate change will render hydrology more difficult as water levels will probably vary more greatly than in the past. Currently, there are several dam projects being completed for electricity generation: the Grand Ethiopian Renaissance Dam will be the largest in the continent when completed. The Grand Inga Dam in the DRC will generate even more capacity, but it is still in the conceptual stages. The EU budgeted some €2,000m. for 2015–20 towards renewable energy projects, while additional assistance valued at €5,000m. was provided by individual EU member states.

Structural transformation involves large-scale changes in the actual make up of a country's or region's production. Such transformation can take decades. The underlying structure of sub-Saharan Africa's economies has not changed dramatically since independence. In 1965 agriculture accounted for 24% of GDP, industry 30% (of which manufacturing comprised 17%) and services 46%, according to the World Bank. By 2015 agriculture contributed 18% of GDP, while industry contributed 25%, manufacturing 11% and services 58%. In 2019 manufacturing as a percentage of GDP remained at 11% for the region. Within the region the distribution of manufacturing activity is highly skewed with just one country, South Africa, accounting for 27.3% of total manufacturing value-added (MVA) in sub-Saharan Africa and registering significant growth over the past two decades. Thus, for most countries there has been a loss in their share of global manufacturing output. However, production costs in the region are generally higher than in other regions. Another problem for the region is the poor level of productivity in general, and of investment productivity in particular, as measured by a capital input-output ratio. Thus, even if Africa can attract more foreign investment, it must make that investment more productive. The region's share of global manufacturing has fallen from a little over 3% in 1970 to less than 3% in 2020. Nonetheless, as more and more production in the global value chain is being divided into distinct tasks carried out by different countries, the region has the potential to take advantage of this shift. It is easier to become proficient in producing one component of a finished good than to produce the final product. However, it is unclear which countries in the region will be able to take advantage of this shift.

Most of the world's advanced nations are often grouped as the 'industrial economies' and their progression from agriculture-based economies to manufacturing- and service-based ones has been seen as key to development strategy. In poor countries structural change—the shift of resources from low productivity to high productivity uses—is a key driver of economic growth. In both theory and practice, industry has been the sector that leads the process of structural change. The East Asian success story is a manufacturing success story. Chile and India have achieved sustained growth through the rapid expansion of agro-industry and services exports, respectively. However, there is a growing body of literature that suggests that this path may no longer be one that can necessarily be followed, as much of the emerging world—including Africa—is facing a problem now known as 'premature deindustrialization': the volume of manufactured exports from many African countries has actually declined and, compared to other developing regions, the share of manufactured goods in total exports is still relatively low.

Furthermore, the region lags behind other developing regions in almost all its industry-related indices. World Bank data indicate that with a few exceptions (Botswana, Cabo Verde, Eswatini, Madagascar, Namibia, Seychelles and South Africa) industrial output per capita as measured by the dollar MVA per population has been stagnant over the past three decades or has even declined. Further analysis by the UN Industrial Development Organization of trends in industrial output suggests that MVA in Africa has grown at a rate exceeding the world average (although falling well short of the phenomenal growth rates achieved in East and South Asia). However, in per head terms, growth in Africa's MVA remains below the global average.

The region annually supplies 10%–15% of the world's petroleum. It should be noted that, with the exception of Congo, Nigeria, Angola,

Gabon and Equatorial Guinea, none of the other states are members of the Organization of Petroleum Exporting Countries (OPEC), and thus are not subject to output limits. Recent discoveries of petroleum, natural gas and minerals in Ghana, Uganda, Kenya, Tanzania and Mozambique have again raised the question of how better to manage the earnings from those resources. A total of 19 African countries are members of the Extractive Industries Transparency Initiative, as discussed in Chapter 2 in this volume, which promotes voluntary standards for showing payments made by companies and revenues collected by governments related to gains from extractive resources. None the less, the oil-rich countries in the region have a poor record of directing such revenues towards social development. For example, the oil producing states of Equatorial Guinea and Gabon, with per head incomes of some US $16,826 and $16,212, respectively, have some of the lowest child immunization rates in the region. The World Bank cited four paradoxes relative to the region's energy crisis: abundant energy but little power; higher prices but high production costs; inefficient reform in the energy sector; and inadequate financing. By mid-2020 international oil prices were at historic lows, trading at times in negative territory (because there was an excess supply and inadequate storage available). Many governments have borrowed heavily against future income from newly discovered oil and gas reserves. On the other hand, for oil importers, lower prices will offer some relief during the COVID-19 pandemic.

While the region lacks some of the information and communication technology available in many other parts of the world (for example, only one African per 100 people had a fixed-line telephone in 2019); between 1999 and 2004 the region's mobile phone market grew faster than in any other region worldwide; and between 2012 and 2013 mobile data use doubled and the region now has 82 mobile phone subscriptions per 100 people (compared to the world average of 106 per 100 people). In 2018 Seychelles had the largest number of mobile phone subscribers per 100 people (at 184), with South Africa next (at 160). Eritrea had the lowest number of mobile phones, with 20 per 100 people. Mobile users in the region prefer to use their devices for a variety of activities that are normally performed on laptops or desktops in industrial countries: mobile phones allow access to banking to people who otherwise would be without it, and provide other important services, such as information on the weather and crop prices. However, internet use is relatively low, with 25% of the population being internet users in 2018 (the world average is 50%). Seychelles has the highest proportion of internet users (59% of the population), followed by South Africa (56%). The region also has the lowest per capita number of households with a computer, at 9.4%, compared to a global average of 44%.

The region's total labour force in 2018 was 428.2m., of whom 46.4% were women. Given the size of the informal sector, as discussed above, estimates for formal sector unemployment vary so greatly that it is impossible to provide precise data, although the World Bank estimated that unemployment in the region for 2019 was 6.1%. It is worth noting, however, that estimates of official unemployment in the formal sector are as high as 30% in some countries, while unofficial estimates are higher still. And, as noted earlier, the informal sector is the main source of employment for most of the region.

Agriculture, food security and the urban bias

Sub-Saharan Africa possesses perhaps one-half of the world's uncultivated land surface and the growth potential in the sector is enormous. According to the World Bank, 'in sub-Saharan Africa, growth in agriculture and services is more effective at reducing poverty than growth in industry'.[8] Unfortunately, a leading factor behind the declines in African economies and the high levels of malnutrition has been the poor performance of agriculture. This sector basically comprises two components: food production for local consumption (often at the subsistence level), and export commodities. Indeed, 90% of the region's agricultural output is produced by smallholders on farms averaging 2.5 ha in size. Agriculture accounts for only 15.6% of GDP for the region as a whole, but for 90% of the rural workforce, two-thirds of total employment and 40% of export earnings. Agricultural labour productivity is quite low, and failure to transform agriculture has resulted in millions of rural Africans being trapped in a cycle of underemployment, underproduction, low incomes and chronic poverty. Access to land (particularly by women, who produce up to 80% of all basic food products) remains a large problem, and insecure land tenure rights prevents farmers from investing in new technology which would increase output. Agricultural productivity is the lowest in the world: value added per worker in 2010 was US $322 compared with the world average of $992. Nevertheless, agriculture was projected to become an industry worth $1,000,000m. by 2030, up from $313,000m. in 2010.

For virtually all African economies the major agricultural exports consist of one, or perhaps two or three, primary products (cash crops such as coffee, tea, sugar, sisal, etc.), the prices of which fluctuate widely from year to year on the world market. Unfortunately, Africa's share of world agricultural exports has declined since the 1970s. Food import costs have increased dramatically, from US $5,433m. in 1980 to $8,352m. in 2000, and averaged some $40,000m. per year by the late 2000s. Commodity prices enjoyed considerable increases prior to the 2008 global financial crisis, and indeed for some years afterwards. However, that boom has now ended. The value of many exports (including oil, gold and coffee) declined between 2014 and 2016. While prices of oil and metals recovered in 2016 and 2017, they fell dramatically in 2019. Indeed, as noted earlier, oil prices are at historic lows.

Food security remains a serious issue for much of the region. Sub-Saharan Africa is the world's most vulnerable area to food insecurity, and acute famine persists in the region. Sub-Saharan Africa has the largest number and highest share of its population food insecure (355m. people, or 35% of the population in 2019). While food security is expected to improve by 2029, according to the United States Department of Agriculture's Economic Research Service, the region will still account for over 70% (287 million people) of the food-insecure people in the developing world.[9] In West Africa, the subregion's largest in terms of both population and GDP, the prevalence of food insecurity is below the regional average, with under 9% of the population projected to be food insecure in 2029. East Africa has the most food insecure people (142m.) but this number is projected to decrease to 90m. by 2029. East Africa is projected to experience similar improvements in food security as West Africa, with the share of population that is food insecure decreasing by about one-half over the next 10 years. Although the smallest subregion measured by population, Central Africa is expected to have the largest number of food insecure people in 2029, increasing by 15% to 93m. However, the proportion of food insecure people is projected to fall from 65% to 60% in the same period. Southern Africa's food security is projected to improve slowly over the next 10 years: the proportion of food insecure people is expected to decrease from 43% to 33%, while the number of food insecure people is projected to decline by 1%, to 61m. people.

While grain production was projected to grow at a little over 2% annually over the next 10 years (through increased productivity and area expansion), this is slower than the increase in demand for grains, which usually increases with rising population and higher incomes. The sub-Saharan African countries are dominated by subsistence-oriented, rain-fed agriculture. One-half of the calories consumed come from grains that are generally rain-fed and thus highly vulnerable to climatic change, which is likely to intensify. Smallholders, who typically grow only one or two crops, are subject to various shocks, including weather and declining commodity prices, and even a modest decline in harvests can be devastating for household food security. Since a large share of family income is spent on food, poor households are vulnerable to food price increases.

Famine can result from several factors, although production failures are perhaps the most common cause. Since 2000 there have been four severe famines—in Ethiopia (in 2000), Malawi (2002), Niger (2005), and in Somalia and Ethiopia (in 2011–12), affecting some 10m. people. In 2015–16 the El Niño drought severely affected large areas in East and Southern Africa. The 2020 locust infestation in East Africa as well as the results of the COVID-19 pandemic will only exacerbate the problem. Another factor can be classified as a response failure by governments and the international community, and can include indifference by governments that, in any event, have a limited capacity to deliver basic services. In addition, many governments have reduced agricultural extension and research services as part of structural adjustments. Finally, poor roads make it difficult for farmers to get their crops to market, and during times of famine present obstacles to the effective distribution of emergency food aid. Few governments have robust early warning systems, or food buffer stocks.

Until quite recently, many governments implemented economic policies that were designed to keep urban wages and living conditions high and farm prices low by maintaining the value of currencies at high, unrealistic rates of exchange. This is understandable and obvious: political power in Africa rests in the city, not in the village or countryside. This 'urban bias'[10] was sometimes a deliberate strategy, at other times more a result of planned rural neglect, and on many occasions was endorsed by the international development community.

In addition to this 'urban bias', producers were often bound by prices fixed by their governments, and at times these 'producer' prices failed to cover input costs. This resulted in farmers reducing their production for sale and reverting to subsistence agriculture. It should be noted that investment in agriculture has traditionally been low. For example, agriculture typically receives less than 10% of public spending. Also, as much as three-quarters of the region's farmland has become degraded owing to erosion and other results of population pressures, resulting, for example, in grain yields stagnating at one metric ton per ha, compared with the world average of about three tons per ha. Productivity growth will require a number of changes. For example, only 4% of the region's cultivated land is irrigated. Improvements in soil fertility, improved seeds and water and pest management have been long overdue. Much-needed spending on research and technology remains low.

Notes

1 P. Nugent, *Africa Since Independence*. Basingstoke: Palgrave Macmillan, 2004.
2 World Bank, *Sub-Saharan Africa from Crisis to Sustainable Growth: A Long-Term Perspective Study*. Washington, DC: World Bank, 1989.
3 World Bank, *Doing Business 2020: Comparing Business Regulation in 190 Economies*. Washington, DC: World Bank, 2020.
4 World Economic Forum, *2019 Competitiveness Report*. Cologny: WEF, 2019.
5 Transparency International, *Corruption Perceptions Index*. Berlin: Transparency International, 2019.
6 UNHCR, *Global Trends At-a-Glance*, 2020. Available at www.unhcr.org/africa.html.
7 World Health Organization, *Preventing and Responding to HIV Drug Resistance in the African Region*. Geneva: WHO, 2020.
8 World Bank, *Africa's Pulse: Decades of Sustained Growth is Transforming Africa's Economies*, Vol. 10. Washington, DC: World Bank, 2014.
9 United States Department of Agriculture, Economic Research Service, *International Food Security Assessment 2019–2027*. Washington, DC: USDA, 2019.
10 M. Lipton, *Why Poor People Stay Poor: Urban Bias in World Development*. Cambridge, MA: Harvard University Press, 1977.

4 The way forward
A transformation?

African governments have responded to increasing pressure from a variety of sources to 'liberalize' their economic policies. During the 1970s and early 1980s the World Bank, the International Monetary Fund (IMF), the United States and other donors began to insist on 'conditionality' for their support. The IMF, in particular, required specific macroeconomic policy changes, usually in the area of exchange rates (i.e. devaluation), and reductions in government spending before a new loan agreement could be granted. Other required measures included the privatization of state-owned enterprises, public sector reform, reduction in the civil service and liberalization of agricultural marketing boards. In 1998 a total of 35 African countries launched structural adjustment programmes or borrowed from the IMF to support reform policies. Although these programmes (subsequently termed Poverty Reduction and Growth Facility and Extended Credit Facility arrangements) have many common points, they are actually varied. Additional pressures, known as the 'Washington Consensus'[1] came from the World Bank and the United States Agency for International Development. Specifically, a landmark 1981 World Bank study proposed four critical policy changes: namely (i) the correction of overvalued exchange rates; (ii) the improvement of price incentives for exports and agriculture; (iii) the protection of industry in a more uniform and less direct way; and (iv) the reduction of direct governmental controls. Other pressures originated and grew internally, as more people became increasingly dissatisfied with their low standard of living and the poor economic performance in their own countries.

Many economists believe that these economic and political reforms did, in general, led to improved economic performance. Indeed, for nearly 20 years starting in the mid-1990s when most of the reforms were robust, most African countries saw strong economic growth and development performance. However, the gains were not equally shared nor was poverty reduced as much as projected or hoped. Furthermore, structural adjustment is very controversial and some studies have failed to demonstrate a definite linkage between reform and growth. Economic assistance to the region has been made increasingly dependent upon economic reform, and the major donor countries of the Organisation for Economic Co-operation and Development (excluding the People's Republic of China) have generally reallocated most of their economic assistance to countries implementing reform programmes. Additionally, the major multilateral donors were also reallocating their resources on this basis.

As sub-Saharan Africa moves forward, its governments have begun to realize that, while many economic problems were inherited, responsibility must be taken for problems that are soluble. Rather than being hostile to foreign investment and entrepreneurs, most African governments are now actively seeking foreign commercial involvement. Certainly, by 2020 many, and perhaps most, African governments are presenting at least the appearance of reform.

During the recent growth period discussed in the Introduction, the region has witnessed perhaps a more sustainable path forward: economic growth is starting to come from other sources (almost one-half of the growth came from the services sector, with a fast-growing middle class). Manufacturing output is expanding as quickly as the rest of the economy. Growth is even faster in services, which expanded at an average rate of 2.6% per person across the region in 1996–2011. Many countries, including Ethiopia, Ghana, Kenya, Mozambique and Nigeria, have recently revised their estimates of gross domestic product to account for their growing non-resource sectors.

As noted in the Introduction, the IMF has projected an economic contraction for the region in 2020 due to the COVID-19 pandemic. However, it also suggests that if successful actions are taken this year (for example, the effectiveness of national disease containment efforts and sufficient support from the international community) growth could recover to 4% in 2021.

In the longer term, there are a number of indicators that suggest the region is poised to effect economic transformation. The African Union (AU) Commission has identified five 'mega trends' that will offer tremendous opportunities (and challenges) for the region:

1   Demographic changes (with a growing young workforce and middle class, greater potential for savings and investment);
2   Rapid urbanization (opportunities for more efficient use of resources and social innovation, with an increasing middle class leading to greater demand);

3 Climate change (potential for new employment in green industries and green technologies);

4 The new 'industrial revolution' (increased efficiencies at the corporate level with lower costs, new innovations in manufacturing, and the growth of niche markets);

5 Shifting terms of trade (increased foreign direct investment (FDI) into the region, transfers of technology and skills, along with diversification of the export market).[2]

In addition to these trends, the region is taking important steps towards greater co-operation and integration. Since most of the region's economies are small, such co-operation is vital to the achievement of enlarged markets, to increase economies of scale and to attract FDI. The most important of these—and another 'game changer'—is the African Continental Free Trade Area (see Chapter 2 in this volume). Most small firms will benefit from reduced tariffs, the harmonization of customs clearance procedures and a lowering of other trade barriers. Furthermore, several regional economic communities are working to strengthen regional value chains and to identify potential regional 'clusters'. For example, the Southern African Development Community's Industrialization Strategy and Roadmap 2015–2063 has prioritized six key clusters.[3] These clusters are selected areas that governments can utilize as a means to focus resources (e.g. infrastructure and financing) and thereby encourage knowledge transfers and other associated spillovers that should enhance countries' specialization and comparative advantages. While such examples of economic clusters are common in the industrial economies (i.e. high technology in California's Silicon Valley or garment manufacturing in northern Italy), they are less common in sub-Saharan Africa. Nonetheless, there are growing examples including Ethiopia's eastern industrial zone and flagship Hawassa Industrial Park, and Rwanda's Kigali special economic zone which have attracted world-class multinational corporations whose operations include textiles, garment manufacturing and shoe production.

Furthermore, the AU Commission lists nine important ongoing pan-African initiatives which could help to usher in economic transformation:

1 Agenda 2063;

2 The AU's Action Plan for the Accelerated Industrial Development of Africa;

3 The United Nations' Third Industrial Development Decade for Africa;

4   The Programme for Infrastructure Development in Africa;
5   The Science, Technology and Innovation Strategy for Africa 2024;
6   The African Agrobusiness and Agro-industries Development Initiative;
7   The Comprehensive Africa Agriculture Development Programme;
8   The African Mining Vision;
9   The African Productive Capacity Initiative.[4]

Given the COVID-19 pandemic it is difficult to say when these initiatives will bear fruit. Nonetheless, this is a resilient region, one with great potential and enormous untapped resources. While there have been setbacks in recent years, there have also been a significant number of positive developments, as discussed above. None the less, it is safe to say that this region is on the verge of effecting economic and social transformation. While it may be difficult to reach this goal, it is attainable.

Notes

1 World Bank, *Accelerated Development in Sub-Saharan Africa: An Agenda for Action*. Washington, DC: World Bank, 1981. (Also known as the Berg Report after its principal author.)
2 African Union, African Development Bank, UN Economic Commission for Africa, *Africa's Development Dynamic: Achieving Productive Transformation*, 2019. It should be noted that these opportunities come with associated risks, including environmental degradation, increased competition from other emerging markets, illicit trade, high youth unemployment, 'brain drain', increased income inequalities, and numerous potential downsides resulting from climate change.
3 Action Plan for SADC Industrialization Strategy and Roadmap. Approved by Summit in Lozitha, Swaziland on 18 March 2017. Available at www.sadc.int/files/2014/6114/9721/Repriting_Final_Strategy_for_translation_051015.pdf.
4 African Union Commission (AUC)/Organisation for Economic Co-operation and Development (OECD), *Africa's Development Dynamics 2019: Achieving Productive Transformation*. Paris: OECD Publishing and Addis Ababa: AUC, 2019. Available at https://doi.org/10.1787/c1cd7de0-en.

Appendix

Table *A1* Countries of Africa South of the Sahara, current GDP (US $ thousands) and population

1	Angola	94,635,415.87	31,825,295
2	Benin	14,390,709.09	11,801,151
3	Botswana	18,340,510.79	2,303,697
4	Burkina Faso	15,745,810.23	20,321,378
5	Burundi	3,012,334.88	11,530,580
6	Cabo Verde	1,981,845.74	549,935
7	Cameroon	38,760,467.03	25,876,380
8	Central African Republic	2,220,307.37	4,745,185
9	Chad	11,314,951.34	15,946,876
10	Comoros	1,185,728.68	850,886
11	Congo, Dem Rep.	47,319,624.20	86,790,567
12	Congo, Rep.	10,820,591.13	5,380,508
13	Côte d'Ivoire	58,792,205.64	25,716,544
14	Equatorial Guinea	11,026,774.95	1,355,986
15	Eritrea	2,065,001.63	3,213,972
16	Eswatini	4,405,405.80	1,148,130
17	Ethiopia	96,107,662.40	112,078,730
18	Gabon	16,657,960.23	2,172,579
19	Gambia, The	1,763,819.05	2,347,706
20	Ghana	6,983,634.22	30,417,856
21	Guinea	13,590,281.81	12,771,246
22	Guinea-Bissau	1,340,389.41	1,920,922
23	Kenya	95,503,088.54	52,573,973
24	Lesotho	2,460,072.44	2,125,268
25	Liberia	3,070,518.10	4,937,374
26	Madagascar	14,083,906.36	26,969,307

27	Malawi	14,083,906.36	18,628,747
28	Mali	14,083,906.36	19,658,031
29	Mauritania	7,593,752.45	4,525,696
30	Mauritius	14,180,444.56	1,265,711
31	Mozambique	14,934,159.93	30,366,036
32	Namibia	12,366,527.72	2,494,530
33	Niger	12,928,145.12	23,310,715
34	Nigeria	448,120,428.86	200,963,599
35	Rwanda	10,122,472.59	12,626,950
36	São Tomé and Príncipe	429,016.61	215,056
37	Senegal	23,578,084.05	16,296,364
38	Seychelles	1,698,843.06	97,625
39	Sierra Leone	3,941,474.31	7,813,215
40	Somalia	917,044.23	15,442,905
41	South Africa	351,431,649.24	58,558,270
42	South Sudan	11,997,800.76	11,062,113
43	Sudan	18,902,284.48	42,813,238
44	Tanzania	63,177,068.17	58,005,463
45	Togo	5,459,979.42	8,082,366
46	Uganda	34,387,229.49	44,269,594
47	Zambia	23,064,722.45	17,861,030
48	Zimbabwe	21,440,758.80	14,645,468

Source: World Bank, *World Development Indicators*, 2020. Available at https://data.worldbank.org/indicator/SP.POP.TOTL.

Bibliography

Acemoglu, D., S. Naidu, P. Restrepo, and J. Robinson (2019) 'Democracy Does Cause Growth', *Journal of Political Economy*, 127(1): 47–100.

Adamopoulos, T., and D. Restuccia (2018) 'Geography and Agricultural Productivity: Cross-Country Evidence from Micro Plot-Level Data', NBER Working Paper 24532, Cambridge, MA: National Bureau of Economic Research.

Adenle, A. A., J. D. Ford, J. Morton, S. Twomlow, K. Alverson, A. Cattaneo, R. Cervigniet al. (2017) 'Managing Climate Change Risks in Africa: A Global Perspective', *Ecological Economics*, 141 (November): 190–201.

Adler, G., R. Duval, D. Furceri, S. K. Çelik, K. Koloskova, and M. Poplawski-Ribeiro (2017) 'Gone with the Headwinds: Global Productivity', IMF Staff Discussion Note 17/04, Washington, DC: International Monetary Fund.

African Development Bank/Organisation for Economic Co-operation and Development/United Nations Development Programme (AfDB/OECD/ UNDP) (2017) *African Economic Outlook 2017: Entrepreneurship and Industrialisation*, Paris: OECD Publishing, http://dx.doi.org/10.1787/a eo-2017-en.

African Union, African Development Bank, and the United Nations Economic Commission for Africa (2020) *Africa Regional Integration Report 2019*, www.integrate-africa.org/fileadmin/uploads/afdb/Documents/ARII-R eport2019-FIN-R40-11jun20.pdf.

African Union, African Development Bank, and the United Nations Economic Commission for Africa (2019) *Africa's Development Dynamic: Achieving Productive Transformation*, www.oecd.org/publications/africa -s-development-dynamics-2019-c1cd7de0-en.htm.

African Union Commission/Organisation for Economic Co-operation and Development (AUC/OECD) (2018) *Africa's Development Dynamics 2018: Growth, Jobs and Inequalities*, Paris: OECD Publishing/Addis Ababa: AUC, https://doi.org/10.1787/9789264302501-en.

Aker, J. C., and I. M. Mbiti (2010) 'Mobile Phones and Economic Development in Africa', *Journal of Economic Perspectives*, 24(3): 207–232.

Arora, V. (2005) 'Economic Growth in Post-Apartheid South Africa: A Growth-Accounting Analysis', in L. A. Ricci and M. Nowak (eds) *Post-Apartheid South Africa: The First Ten Years*, Washington, DC: International Monetary Fund, pp. 13–22.

Ayyagari, M., P. F. Juarros, M. S. Martinez Peria, and S. Singh (2016) 'Access to Finance and Job Growth: Firm-Level Evidence Across Developing Countries', Policy Research Working Paper 7604, Washington, DC: World Bank.

Bah, E., and L. Fang (2015) 'Impact of the Business Environment on Output and Productivity in Africa', *Journal of Development Economics*, 114 (May): 159–171.

Barofsky, J., T. D. Anekwe, and C. Chase (2015) 'Malaria Eradication and Economic Outcomes in Sub-Saharan Africa: Evidence from Uganda', *Journal of Health Economics*, 44 (December): 118–136.

Barrett, C. B., L. Christiaensen, M. Sheahan, and A. Shimeles (2017) 'On the Structural Transformation of Rural Africa', Policy Research Working Paper 7938, Washington, DC: World Bank.

Beegle, K., and L. Christiaensen (2019) *Accelerating Poverty Reduction in Africa*, Washington, DC: World Bank.

Blimpo, M. P., and M. Cosgrove-Davies (2019) *Electricity Access in Sub-Saharan Africa: Uptake, Reliability, and Complementary Factors for Economic Impact*, Washington, DC: World Bank.

Bloom, D. E., M. Kuhn, and K. Prettner (2017) 'Africa's Prospects for Enjoying a Demographic Dividend', *Journal of Demographic Economics*, 83 (1): 63–76.

Calderón, C., and S. Boreux (2016) 'Citius, Altius, Fortius: Is Growth in Sub-Saharan Africa More Resilient?', *Journal of African Economies*, 25(4): 502–528.

Calderón, C., and C. Cantú (2019) 'Trade Integration and Growth: Evidence from Sub-Saharan Africa', Policy Research Working Paper 8859, Washington, DC: World Bank.

Calderón, C., and L. Servén (2010) 'Infrastructure and Economic Development in Sub-Saharan Africa', *Journal of African Economies*, 19(S1): i13–i87.

Callaghy, T. M. and J. Ravenhill (eds) (1993) *Hemmed In: Responses to Africa's Economic Decline*, New York: Columbia University Press.

Chen, C., and D. Restuccia (2018) 'Agricultural Productivity Growth in Africa', Background paper prepared for the AFRCE project Boosting Productivity in Sub-Saharan Africa, Washington, DC: World Bank.

Choi, J., M. Dutz, and Z. Usman (2019) *The Future of Work in Africa: Harnessing the Potential of Digital Technologies for All*, Washington, DC: World Bank.

Collier, P., G. Conway, and T. Venables (2008) 'Climate Change and Africa', *Oxford Review of Economic Policy*, 24(2): 337–353.

Corrigan, T. (2017) 'Rethinking Infrastructure in Africa: A Governance Approach', Occasional Paper 252, Johannesburg: South African Institute of International Affairs.

De Vries, G. J., M. P. Timmer, and K. de Vries (2013) '*Structural Transformation in Africa: Static Gains, Dynamic Losses*', GGDC Research Memorandum 136, Groningen: Groningen Growth and Development Centre, University of Groningen.

Dowden, R. (2009) *Africa: Altered States, Ordinary Miracles*, London: Portobello Books.

Du Plessis, S., and B. Smit (2007) 'South Africa's Growth Revival after 1994', *Journal of African Economies*, 16(5): 668–704.

Easterly, W. (2007) *The White Man's Burden: Why the West's Efforts to Aid the Rest Have Done So Much Ill and So Little Good*, Oxford: Oxford University Press.

Eden, M., and H. Nguyen (2016) '*Reconciling Micro- and Macro-Based Estimates of Technology Adoption Lags in a Model of Endogenous Technology Adoption*', in J. T. Araujo, E. Vostroknutova, K. Wacker, and M. Clavijo (eds) *Understanding the Income and Efficiency Gap in Latin America and the Caribbean*, Washington, DC: World Bank.

Elbadawi, I., and N. Loayza (2008) 'Informality, Employment and Economic Development in the Arab World', *Journal of Development and Economic Policies*, 10(2): 27–75.

Elekdag, S., D. Muir, and Y. Wu (2015) 'Trade Linkages, Balance Sheets, and Spillovers: The Germany-Central European Supply Chain', *Journal of Policy Modeling*, 37(2): 374–387.

Elgin, C., and O. Oztunali (2012) 'Shadow Economies Around the World: Model Based Estimates', Working Paper 2012/05, İstanbul: Boğaziçi University, Department of Economics.

Enache, M., E. Ghani, and S. O'Connell (2016) '*Structural Transformation in Africa: A Historical View*', Policy Research Working Paper 7743, Washington, DC: World Bank.

Food and Agriculture Organization of the United Nations (FAO) (2019) *Crop Prospects and Food Situation*, July, Rome: FAO.

Fosu, A. K., and A. F. Abass (2019) 'Domestic Credit and Export Diversification: Africa from a Global Perspective', *Journal of African Business*, 20 (2): 160–179.

Freund, C., M. J. Ferrantino, M. Maliszewska, and M. Ruta (2018) 'Impacts on Global Trade and Income of Current Trade Disputes', MTI Practice Note 2, Washington, DC: World Bank.

Goedhuys, M., N. Janz, and P. Mohnen (2008) 'What Drives Productivity in Tanzanian Manufacturing Firms: Technology or Business Environment?', *European Journal of Development Research*, 20(2): 199–218.

Groth, H., and J. F. May (eds) (2017) *Africa's Population: In Search of a Demographic Dividend*, Cham: Springer International.

Haile, F. (2018) 'Structural Change in West Africa: A Tale of Gain and Loss', Policy Research Working Paper 8336, Washington, DC: World Bank.

Hjort, J., and J. Poulsen (2019) 'The Arrival of Fast Internet and Employment in Africa', *American Economic Review*, 109(3): 1032–1079.

Intergovernmental Panel on Climate Change (IPCC) (2014) *Climate Change 2014: Impacts, Adaptation, and Vulnerability*, IPCC Working Group II, Geneva: IPCC.

International Monetary Fund (IMF) (2019) *World Economic Outlook*, April, Washington, DC: IMF, www.imf.org/external/pubs/ft/weo/2019/01/weodata/index.aspx (accessed 23 May 2019).

Khadiagala, G. M. (2015) 'Global and Regional Mechanisms for Governing the Resource Curse in Africa', *Politikonj: South Africa Journal of Political Studies*, 42(1).

Kim, Y. E., N. V. Loayza, and C. Meza-Cuadra (2016) 'Productivity as the Key to Economic Growth and Development', Research & Policy Brief 3, Washington, DC: World Bank.

Kouassi, R. (2015) *L'Afrique: un géant qui refuse de naître—La solution, c'est de tout reprendre à zéro*, Paris: L'Harmattan.

Kose, M. A., and F. Ohnsorge (2019) *A Decade since the Global Recession: Lessons and Challenges for Emerging and Developing Economies*, Washington, DC: World Bank.

La Porta, R., and A. Scheifler (2014) 'Informality and Development', *Journal of Economic Perspectives*, 28(3): 109–126.

Lederman, D., and W. F. Maloney (2007) *Natural Resources: Neither Curse nor Destiny*, Palo Alto, CA: Stanford University Press.

Lipton, M. (1977) *Why Poor People Stay Poor: Urban Bias in World Development*, Cambridge, MA: Harvard University Press.

Meredith, M. (2006) *The State of Africa*, London: Simon & Schuster.

Moyo, D. (2010) *Dead Aid: Why Aid Is Not Working and How There Is Another Way for Africa*, London: Penguin.

Ndikumama, L. and Boyce, J. K. (2012) 'Rich Presidents of Poor Nations: Capital Flight from Resource-Rich Countries in Africa', *ACAS Bulletin*, 87.

Nugent, P. (2004) *Africa Since Independence*, Basingstoke: Palgrave Macmillan.

Oosthuizen, M., K. Lilenstein, F. Steenkamp, and A. Cassim (2016) 'Informality and Inclusive Growth in Sub-Saharan Africa', ELLA Regional Evidence Paper, Lima: ELLA Network.

Organisation for Economic Co-operation and Development (OECD) (2019) *Development Aid at a Glance*, Paris: OECD Publishing.

Organisation for Economic Co-operation and Development/African Union Commission/ African Tax Administration Forum (OECD/AUC/ATAF) (2018) *Revenue Statistics in Africa 2018*, Paris: OECD Publishing, https://doi.org/10.1787/9789264305885-en-fr.

Organisation for Economic Co-operation and Development Assistance Committee (OECD-DAC) (2018a) *International Development Statistics*, www.oecd.org/dac/stats/idsonline.htm (accessed 11 May 2019).

Organisation for Economic Co-operation and Development Assistance Committee (OECD-DAC) (2018b) *Country Programmable Aid*, www.oecd.org/dac/financing-sustainable-development/development-finance-standards/cpa.htm.

Raballand, G., S. Refas, M. Beuran, and G. Isik (2012) *Why Does Cargo Spend Weeks in Sub-Saharan African Ports? Lessons from Six Countries.* Washington, DC: World Bank.

Rodrik, D. (1999) 'Where Did All the Growth Go? External Shocks, Social Conflict, and Growth Collapses', *Journal of Economic Growth*, 4(4): 385–412.

Rodrik, D. (2016a) 'Premature Deindustrialization', *Journal of Economic Growth*, 21(1): 1–33.

Rodrik, D. (2016b) 'An African Growth Miracle?', *Journal of African Economies*, 27(1): 10–27.

Sparks, D. L. (2016a) 'The Sustainable Development Goals and Agenda 2063: Implications for Economic Integration in Africa', *Research in Applied Economics*, 8(4): 12–40.

Sparks, D. L. (2016b) 'Preventing Premature Deindustrialization in Sub-Saharan Africa: The Importance of the Road Transportation Sector', *Advances in Social Sciences Research Journal*, 3(3), https://doi.org/10.14738/assrj.33.1906.

Sparks, D. L. (2013) 'Will Sub-Saharan Africa Meet the Millennium Development Goals and Does it Matter?', *Research in Applied Economics*, 5(1): 98–107.

Sparks, D. L. (2012) 'Large Scale Land Acquisitions in Sub-Saharan Africa: The New Scramble?', *International Business and Economic Research Journal*, 11(6): 687–696.

Sparks, D. L. (2011) 'India and China's Growing Economic Involvement in Sub-Saharan Africa', *Journal of African Studies and Development*, 3(4).

Sparks, D. L. (with Steve Barnett) (2010) 'The Informal Sector in Sub-Saharan Africa: Out of the Shadows to Foster Sustainable Employment and Equity?', *International Business and Economics Research Journal*, 9(5): 1–11.

Sparks, D. L. (2008) 'Electronic Payments in Sub Saharan Africa: Will Mobile Telephony Accounts Systems be the Next Leapfrog Technology for Development?', *International Review of Business Research Papers*, 4(1): 325–336.

Sparks, D. L. (with Richard Dutu) (2004) 'The Future of Monetary Integration in Southern Africa: Lessons from the European Monetary Union?', *Journal of African Policy Studies*, 10(1): 19–53.

Sparks, D. L. (2003a) 'Globalization and Sub-Saharan Africa: Will the Promise of Shared Prosperity Ever be Realized?', *Journal of African Policy Studies*, 9(1): 71–81. (First published in The Proceedings of Annual Research Conference, American University in Cairo, Cairo, pp. 49–58.)

Sparks, D. L. (2003b) 'The Future of Monetary Integration in Southern Africa: Should SADC Join the Rand Monetary Area?', in M. Malliaris, and M. Anastasios (eds) *The Global Economy: Financial, Monetary, Trade and Knowledge Asymmetries*, Toronto: APF Press, pp. 110–125.

Taylor, I. (2016) 'Dependency Redux: Why Africa Is Not Rising', *Review of African Political Economy*, 43, 147.

Transparency International (2019) *Corruption Perceptions Index 2018*, London: Transparency International.

Udry, Christopher (2010) 'The Economics of Agriculture in Africa: Notes Toward a Research Program', *African Journal of Agricultural and Resource Economics*, 5(1): 284–299.

United Nations Economic Commission for Africa/African Union Commission/African Development Bank (ECA/AUC/AfDB) (2010) *Assessing Regional Integration in Africa IV: Enhancing Intra-African Trade*, Addis Ababa: United Nations Economic Commission for Africa, www.uneca.org/sites/default/files/PublicationFiles/aria4full.pdf.

Young, Tom (2018) *Neither Devil Nor Child*, London: One World.

World Economic Forum/World Bank/African Development Bank (WEF/WB/AfDB) (2017) *The Africa Competitiveness Report 2017: Addressing Africa's Demographic Dividend*, Geneva: World Economic Forum, www3.weforum.org/docs/WEF_ACR_2017.pdf.

World Bank (2020) *Doing Business 2020: Comparing Business Regulations in 190 Economies*, Washington, DC: World Bank.

World Bank (2019a) *World Development Indicators*, http://datatopics.worldbank.org/world-development-indicators/ (accessed 11 May 2019).

World Bank (2019b) *Exporter Dynamics Database*, http://microdata.worldbank.org/index.php/catalog/2545/study-description (accessed 25 February 2019).

World Bank (2019c) *Boosting Productivity in Sub-Saharan Africa*, Washington, DC: World Bank.

World Bank (2019d) *Global Economic Prospects: Darkening Skies*, January, Washington, DC: World Bank.

World Bank (2019e) *World Development Report 2020: Trading for Development in the Age of Global Value Chains*, Washington, DC: World Bank.

World Bank (2018) *Global Economic Prospects: The Turning of the Tide?* June, Washington, DC: World Bank.

World Bank (2017a) *Global Investment Competitiveness Report 2017/2018: Foreign Investor Perspectives and Policy Implications*, Washington, DC: World Bank, https://openknowledge.worldbank.org/bitstream/handle/10986/28493/9781464811753.pdf.

World Bank (2017b) *Doing Business 2018: Reforming to Create Jobs*, Washington, DC: World Bank.

World Bank (2016a) *Africa's Pulse: An Analysis of Issues Shaping Africa's Economic Future*, October, Washington, DC: World Bank.

World Bank (2016b) *Africa's Pulse: Decades of Sustained Growth is Transforming Africa's Economies*, 10. 2014.

World Bank (1989) *Sub-Saharan Africa from Crisis to Sustainable Growth: A Long-Term Perspective Study*, Washington, DC: World Bank.

World Bank (1981) *Accelerated Development in Sub-Saharan Africa: An Agenda for Action*, Washington, DC: World Bank.

Index

CPSIA information can be obtained
at www.ICGtesting.com
Printed in the USA
BVHW090444221022
649997BV00015B/1054

9 781032 034591